Larry Cunningham

A Showband Legend

Tom Gilmore

MENTOR
BOOKS

First published in 2009 by

MENTOR BOOKS

43 Furze Road
Sandyford Industrial Estate
Dublin 18
Republic of Ireland

Tel: +353 1 295 2112 / 3 Fax: +353 1 295 2114
Email: admin@mentorbooks.ie
www.mentorbooks.ie

ISBN: 978 - 1 - 906623 - 39 - 5

A catalogue record for this book is available from the British Library

Editor: Treasa O'Mahony
Book design, typesetting and cover design: Kathryn O'Sullivan

Printed in Ireland by ColourBooks Ltd
1 3 5 7 9 10 8 6 4 2

Contents

Acknowledgements

Larry Cunningham

I would like to acknowledge the efforts of my late parents, Michael and Julia Cunningham, and my late brothers, Michael and Eugene, in the formative years of my showband career. Thanks are also due to my sisters Anna, Sheila, Kathleen and Breda. To my wife Beatrice, our children – Regina, Sinéad, Lorcán and Barry and our grandchildren – Molly and Peter Sheridan, my sincere gratitude for their continuing support, love and understanding.

I greatly appreciate contributions made to my career by all the members of the Grafton and Mighty Avons showbands and the Country Blue Boys, living and deceased. To my managers mentioned in this book, some of whom have also sadly passed away, I owe a debt of gratitude.

Thanks also to Chuck Owens, June McLoughlin, Billy Faughnan, Johnny Doran, Mary O'Connor, Margo O'Donnell, Francis Canning, the Star Trek band, Breege, Eddie, Sean and Valerie Quinn, the Country Gold band, Simon Commins, Sean Furlong, Eddie Rowe, Eddie Cahill, Keith Donnelly, Pat Hayes, Joe Bradley, Tommy Doyle as well as Gerard and Steve of Country Harmony.

I would also like to acknowledge the efforts of all the producers who worked with me over the years, in particular Noel Kelehan, Bill O'Donovan, Tommy Ellis, Crawford Bell, the late Dermot O'Brien and, in more recent times, Jonathan Owens. Thanks also to the producer of the 'Ballyjamesduff Frolics' show, John McBrien, who wrote a number of songs I recorded, including 'Tribute to JFK' and 'Ramblin' Irishman'. I remember with fondness the many promoters who have helped me over the years including those who have passed away: Bill Fuller, Jim Aiken, Noel Henry, Tommy Kiernan and Tommy Quinn.

Many other promoters also helped my career including Albert and Jim Reynolds, Gertie Burns (USA), John and Michael Burns (London), Peggy McCabe (Manchester), Gerry Flynn of the Enjoy Travel company, David Hull Promotions (Belfast), Shaun Wallace, Billy Morrissey Promotions, Joe Finnegan from Shannonside Radio, Declan Nerney and Frank Kilbride, Hooley Promotions, Pio McCann, Highland Radio, Willie Carty Promotions, Connie Lynch, Pat Hayes as well as Noel, Tommy and Mattie Henry of Celtic Blues. I would also like to thank all the radio and TV presenters and production people as well as members of the press for publicity over the years, including Gay Byrne and his wife Kathleen Watkins for airplays on Radio Éireann in the early days, as well as Jimmy Magee, Terry Wogan, Larry Gogan and many other DJs.

A special word of thanks to Mary Kennedy and Val Fitzpatrick of Fitzpatrick's Céilí House, Mohill, County Leitrim for their invaluable assistance in providing press cuttings and photographs of the late Phil Fitzpatrick who wrote 'Lovely Leitrim'.

Acknowledgements

Tom Gilmore

I would like to thank Larry and Beatrice Cunningham who were most cooperative when researching this book. Particular thanks go to Sinéad without whom the whole project would never have happened.

I would also like to mention Ann, Raymond, Louise and Matthew Quirke who have always been there when often needed over the years. To the extended Collins families in Chester and in particular to William and Becky, thanks for their love and inspiration.

My gratitude also to the extended Gilmore families in Counties Galway and Cork and to all others, friends and neighbours, who encouraged this project, especially David Burke, Editor, and my colleagues in *The Tuam Herald*, including John Dooley who screened all the photographs, and all in Galway Bay FM Radio.

To the publishing company Mentor Books, in particular Danny McCarthy and Editor Treasa O'Mahony, thank you for having faith in this project.

Sincere thanks to Jimmy Magee, Daniel O'Donnell and Mick Clerkin for their cooperation and for sharing their memories for this book. Also to the International Ambassador of Country Music, George Hamilton IV, for his kind comments.

Foreword

One can say with conviction that Larry Cunningham was among the first few singing stars from the showband scene to popularise Country music in Ireland.

Larry will always be identified with singing the songs of Jim Reeves but his own distinctive voice made him instantly recognisable. From the moment you hear him sing the first lines of his biggest hit 'Lovely Leitrim', you realise that Larry always had the definitive version of that song.

Of course this was only one of Larry's many hits. Years later I recorded some of the songs that he had popularised during his long and illustrious showbusiness career. Those songs included 'Among the Wicklow Hills' and 'Pretty Little Girl from Omagh' along with several others.

From an early age I was aware that Larry was a big singing star and I often listened to his records. I met Larry when my sister Margo and himself had a hit with the song 'Yes Mr Peters' and they worked together on the showband scene for some time in the mid 1970s.

When I lived in Dublin in my late teens and early twenties, I often danced to Larry and his band in ballrooms such as The Olympic, The Ierne and the Irish Club. My memories of those dances are that Larry had a unique smooth-sounding Country voice and he always had a great dance band with him.

This book is filled with nostalgia as Larry looks back on his life. It will strike a chord with anyone who has lived through the showband era and beyond. There is a lot of wry humour in it too – obviously Larry never took the showbusiness tag too seriously.

He was a singing star of international standing and he was among the select few from the showband scene who laid the foundations for many of us to enjoy success singing Country and Irish songs in the decades since his formative years on the music circuit.

At times it has been a rollercoaster on the showbusiness scene for Larry Cunningham but he has obviously enjoyed the ride. Now you can enjoy the read!

Daniel O'Donnell, August 2009.

Dedications

I wish to dedicate this book to the memory of my parents, the late Katie (Lally) Gilmore (1920–2008) and the late William Gilmore (1919–1986).

I also dedicate it to you, the reader – I hope you enjoy this trip back in time through some of the heady days and nights of the showband era in Ireland and abroad.

Tom Gilmore

In the early days of the International Festivals of Country Music at Wembley I remember Larry Cunningham as one of the Irish artists who stood out and his singing style made an instant impression on me.

Larry seemed to be popular with the British fans as well as with the Irish contingent at Wembley.

One of my memories is of Murray Cash introducing him to the crowd and referring to Larry as the Jim Reeves of Ireland.

Of course Jim was known as Gentleman Jim and later when I got to meet Larry my first impression was that he was a real Irish gentleman. Gentleman Larry would be an apt title for him.

George Hamilton IV, Nashville. Tennesee

One
A Singer - Not by Choice

I am very proud of my Daddy's name
Although his kind of music and mine
Ain't exactly the same.

'Family Tradition' – Hank Williams Junior

It was a night in the bleak mid-February of 1938. Longford mother, Julia Cunningham, gave birth to a baby who could have been destined to become a priest, if he followed one family tradition. Even though the date of Larry Cunningham's birth may have been changed, it did not mean that he was to become, as his mother hoped, a cleric. Larry first saw the light of day in 1938 on 13 February – or was he born on the following day? Perhaps a song that Larry later wrote, though set in County Kerry, suggests a scene similar to the one near Granard, County Longford where he was born.

I was born in sweet Killarney, one day when I was young
And that's the very reason why the Blarney's on my tongue.
Oh! The night was cold and stormy and the rain came pouring down
And the old nurse Judy Kearney lived a long way out of town.

'They Wouldn't Do It Now' – Larry Cunningham

Obviously Larry doesn't remember being born! But perhaps what he was told by others around him influenced him to write that popular song. His father was Michael Cunningham and his mother was Julia Cosgrove. She came from the Leitrim border area near Ballinamuck, County Longford. It seems that Julia hoped her bouncing baby boy would grow up to be a priest.

Change of Birth Date

Larry confirms that, similar to the family that he and his wife Beatrice have, his mother also came from a family of two boys and two girls.

'My grandfather, on my mother's side had two sons and one was a top class step dancer who had won medals all over the place. The other son was a great fiddle player and he became a priest. Apart from his work as a priest he was a multi-talented musician and a craftsman as well. He made his own fiddle and we still have it in the family today,' says Larry.

'His name was Larry and I was named after him as they thought I would be a priest too. Indeed when I was a kid I often told people that I was going to be a priest.' Larry also refers to this in a book written by RTÉ broadcaster Brian Carthy. 'My early childhood ambition was to be a priest'. (*The A to Z of Country & Irish Stars* – Gill & Macmillan 1991, p.41)

'All three previous generations of my mother's family had sons who were priests and all were named Larry.' Perhaps Julia's hopes of him being a priest too was the reason why his time of birth is listed as before midnight on February 13th. This seems to have paved the way for him to be christened Larry, as that name had been a good luck omen for priests in previous generations. 'I believe I was born in the early hours of February 14th, St Valentine's Day. But my mother may have said that I was born just before midnight. So instead of naming me Val she decided that I was to be called Larry.'

Later in life, similar to Jesus, the teenage Larry became a carpenter. But singing, and not preaching, was what took him along the road to fame. Yet singing was something he shunned when success first beckoned and being a carpenter or a woodwork teacher then seemed better career options to him.

As his strange showbusiness story unfolds one can detect some regrets from his utterances that he did not choose a career of chalk and talk, blackboards and benches. However, regrets don't surface regarding his shunning of a religious career route. But later on in life he recalls comments by controversial cleric, the late Fr Michael Cleary, about one benefit of being a man of the cloth. Singing on stage, rather that preaching from a church pulpit, was to be the way Larry Cunningham carried on a family tradition.

Larry's father was a farmer. But their farm was not very big, approximately 40 to 50 acres. There were seven children in the Cunningham family, four girls and three boys and he was the second youngest. For a time there was an elderly aunt and an elderly workman also living with them. 'We cared for them and this brought the number in the family up to 11 at one stage,' Larry recalls. 'You can imagine my mother having to cook, bake and wash for that number of people – but she managed,' he adds.

'Unfortunately my two brothers, Eugene and Michael, are no longer with us as they passed away all too young.' His four sisters are still alive – Kathleen, Sheila, Anna and Breeda. Larry says his parents were very organised with their work and all the different farm tasks revolved around the four seasons of the year. 'They had a season for everything; they carried out all the work on the farm along those lines. While nobody had much money they seemed to manage and our home was a very happy one,' he recounts. The Cunningham's home was one of the few in his village that was not thatched when he was a child. 'Our house had a tiled roof when we were growing up but I understand that this replaced a previous thatched one,' says Larry.

Getting a 'Round Sound' at School

About 100 yards from the dilapidated Clooneen primary school there is a left turn off the main road down a twisty, winding, narrower road. This leads to the house where Larry was born and reared. His ancestral home is still there in the heartland of rural Ireland. On schooldays Larry and his siblings walked over two miles along this twisting narrow road, little better than a dirt track, to the small school.

As he visits the school now Larry looks around the semi-derelict building and one detects sadness in his voice as he stands inside the derelict front hall.

'We would hang up our coats there after walking the two miles from my home to the school. I don't remember my first day at school very well but I do remember that I did not want to come here,' he reminisces. 'However, after a while when I got to know all my pals I came to like the days we spent here. We walked barefoot to and from school in summer. Most days I brought a bottle of milk and some slices of soda bread that my mother would bake.'

Now the plaster is falling from the walls. The ceilings and floorboards are rotting and the stench of damp and decay is everywhere at Clooneen NS. According to an engraving on a stone over the school's front door it was established in 1895. No doubt it had its glory days, but this dirty grey building is now a sorry sight. Larry falters in his footing as one of the dirty rotting floorboards gives way under him. He is walking around inside his old school for the first time in years and perhaps he is saddened at its sorry state today. The silence is deafening in this damp, dreary, dirty building. The scene now is far removed from the days of yesteryear when the school buzzed with the sounds of children as busy as bees around a hive. Larry says his older brothers and sisters paved the way for him to start his days as a pupil at Clooneen NS. He took his younger sister there for the first day of her formal education a few years later. He often carried sods of turf to school for burning in the fires that heated the classrooms. But sometimes the arrival of fuel helped him and his pals avoid a few classes. That was when some parents brought carts of turf to the school and the boys would have to stack up the fuel in the shed.

He speaks with fondness about one of the teachers, Mrs Brady, who was from Granard. He also remembers a one-time teacher at the school – a 'Master Cassidy' – who invented a threshing machine. This was operated by some of the teacher's sons around local farms.

Larry also remembers being in the school choir, sitting on a long forum with others in his class. He says the teacher, Miss Mullen, would write songwords in Irish and English on the blackboard. He admits that these were his first formal music lessons and the teacher would often correct the pupils on pronunciations. That memory floods back to him as he stands in the now crumbling school building and he bursts into song.

We are the boys of Wexford
Who fought with heart and hand.

'According to the teacher we should give "round sound" to the word "boys". She was strict, perhaps a tough teacher, but she was always good and fair,' he adds.

Playing for Pennies

Aside from school, it was among the smoky firesides of the stone-walled, whitewashed cottages of the 1940s that the fledgling singer Larry Cunningham was infected with the music bug. In earlier times the fiddle tunes and songs from the midlands of Ireland were taken to America and intertwined with other influences to form bluegrass music. These tunes were also handed down to the Cunningham and Cosgrove clans at home. Some were eventually honed into showband career songs by the once reluctant singer, Larry.

According to Paddy Moloney of the Chieftains, the origins of 'the country music anthem of Texas' are Irish. Perhaps bluegrass music, similar to Larry's family, originated in the Irish midlands! Paddy claims that 'Cotton-Eyed Joe' is the Texas country music anthem and in reality it is an old Irish traditional reel called 'The Mountain Top'. 'Did you wash your father's shirt, and did you wash it clean?' These were the words in the old Irish tune that evolved into 'Cotton-Eyed Joe' according to Paddy (*Blackwell Guide to Recorded Country Music* – 1993, p.9). Paddy recalls that as a child he first heard his grandmother play this reel in her home near the Sliabh Bloom Mountains in the midlands of Ireland.

Back when he was growing up, not far from the Sliabh Bloom Mountains, Larry Cunningham says all his brothers and sisters were musical. So also were his parents and grandparents.

'I am not joking when I say that every one of my brothers and sisters could sing as good, if not better than I could. But I suppose compared to how I sounded when I started off I improved a bit as time went by – but I needed to improve,' laughs Larry. 'If my brothers and sisters had got the same chance as I got, if they got as lucky as I did in the music business, they had the qualities to be entertainers too. When we were all playing traditional Irish music around home we did this for the love of it and not for money. At no time were any of us looking towards music as a possible career.' He claims his background in traditional music and songs was influenced by Leitrim and Longford styles. His mother grew up near the border of Longford and Leitrim and this resulted in the family being interested in songs from both counties.

'My grandfather, on my mother's side, and all his people were fiddle players and flute players. So it was possibly from there that the music started out for me. But my father was musical too and he had a good singing voice and could also play the accordion. He was a highly educated man and almost every day people would be calling to our house for him to sign all sorts of official forms for grants, medical assistance etc. I think every parish had somebody like my father who people could go to for filling in forms at that time.

'My mother would attend music sessions in the homes of members of her family and later as I grew up we would have sessions at home. Lord have mercy on my grandfather, Michael Cosgrove – when he was alive he would come up here and he would bring his tin whistle. He would take it out and start to play and I would take out the fiddle and we would have a session,' he says. 'As a child I remember music being played regularly in our house. One of the local lads, a fantastic accordion player, would often play music with me, if we had a dance in our home. He was Micky Blaney. Lord rest him now as he has passed away. He influenced me at an early age; when I was just 10 or 11 years old, he was brilliant on the accordion. I would be playing the tin whistle and he would be on the accordion.' The two pals would get together for music sessions in the Cunningham home regularly. 'But sometimes we were told to go outside the door when the older people did not like some of the stuff that we were playing. But other times when I was playing the fiddle and he was still on the accordion they would invite people to the house to hear us playing.'

The two would often play at house dances. For the fun of it they also went around with the wren. This is an old Irish custom of musicians going from door to door on St Stephen's Day and playing for a few coins. Larry laughs as he remembers the success of this latter activity of busking on people's doorsteps. 'We earned what we thought was an absolute fortune doing that.' Unwittingly this rural kid from Longford was taking tentative steps towards entertaining thousands of fans at venues such as Carnegie Hall or the Wembley Arena. As he learned some of the old traditional tunes Larry was often asked to perform at local concerts, usually playing either the tin whistle or the fiddle. Larry can thank the success of his local football team for the opportunity to make his debut as singer. But it was a far cry from the grandeur of Carnegie Hall, Wembley or Nashville's Grand Ole Opry.

Teenage Singing Star!

Near Cloonagh NS in Longford there still stands a nondescript grey concrete building with a semi-circular roof, like those you might see on old-style haysheds around rural Ireland. This is where Larry made his first stage appearance as a child singing a football song.

'This is the other end of Mullinalaghta parish. This is the area that has our local church where I was baptised. That's the graveyard there where I have my plot booked for when I pass on,' says Larry as we drive through this part of the parish. It also has two pubs, Cloonagh School and of course the hall where he made his first singing appearance at about 12 years of age.

The hall was used for many activities. Bazaars were held here and it was a hive of activity – especially during the seven weeks of Lent. During that time many parish groups including the local football club could make a few pounds from the various activities at the hall.

The teacher at that end of the parish, the late Pat Murphy, was a pillar of the community according to Larry. 'He was a brilliant human being and perhaps it was only when he passed on that people realised just how much of an asset he was to the whole area. He was a fantastic singer, a great teacher and unbelievably talented as a drama producer. There was no year that I remember during my childhood that he did not come up with a new drama production for Lent. Sometimes he would have sketches that he had written himself. Master Murphy would also put on some well-known plays, sometimes ones that were difficult to act in. But he was one man who could act and produce almost anything. He would get all the local children in his part of the parish involved and then he would come up to our end of the area. That is how I got selected to join one of the Black and White Minstrels shows that he was producing.' Larry recalls that some children in these shows were no more than seven or eight years of age at that time. But they were all confident going out on stage as part of a group – because 'Master Murphy' was in charge.

The football team in Mullinalaghta went through a purple patch during this time, which gave him his first taste of performing as a singer. They beat a team named The Wanderers, who were the big stars in Longford then. This was a massive success for football players from a small rural area. Larry says that after Mullinalaghta won their first of three championships and seven Leader cups (sponsored by *The Longford Leader* newspaper), everybody was shouting 'come on the half parish'. It was for a concert during Lent, a few months after the club won the county football championship that teacher Pat Murphy wrote a song about the team. He chose Larry to sing it at an event to celebrate the football success in the local hall. The cup, with the football on top of it, had pride of place on the table in the parish hall and it stood taller than the guest singer! Larry was barely a teenager but he still vividly remembers the scene as he got his first big break to sing on stage. 'That was my first introduction to showbusiness,' recalls Larry as he spontaneously bursts into a few lines of the song, reliving those childhood memories.

It was on a stormy Sunday
We took old Longford town
And there we played the Wanderers
A team of great renown
Johnny Dunne of Galway
He refereed the game
The day that Mullinalaghta
Made their football name and fame.

'There must have been 15 verses in the song and I had to sing it at many other functions in the area after that. But I remember that one of the lads, who was a star on the team, was not mentioned in the song and he was a relation of ours. My father stopped me from singing the song until they added a verse with that player's name in it,' admits Larry. When he was making his singing debut in this local parish hall Larry was also nearing the end of his primary education at Clooneen NS.

To Teach or Not to Teach

Larry suggests that even though he had great respect for his primary schoolteacher, Miss Mullen, perhaps she did too many subjects through the medium of Irish. This made it difficult for him and others when they moved on to Granard Vocational School. 'I nearly needed an interpreter then as I had done so much work in primary school *as Gaeilge*. My maths was all done through the medium of Irish and maths was important for woodwork and mechanical drawing, which I wanted to study. But she was a brilliant teacher and I left there at 13 years old with a good basic education,' he adds.

At that time many students only needed to spend two years in a vocational school before going out into the world of work to become apprentices in the trade of their choice.

Dan Kennedy was one teacher during Larry's days in Granard Vocational School who had a profound impact on him. 'He asked me and another pal of mine, Phil Donoghue, to stay on for an extra year at the school and this was not usually done. That extra year resulted in us being able to go on to Dublin to study a short course there. This qualified us as manual instructors. We could then teach woodwork, mechanical drawing and maths,' says Larry. It was a time when some young people were only going to vocational schools to do carpentry or metalwork. Many pupils wanted to avoid studying subjects such as Irish and English, which were the big ones in other schools. But then the Vocational Schools started putting more emphasis on academic subjects as well. 'I'm not sure if that was a good or bad idea, as some students would stay away the days they had to do Irish. Sometimes this resulted in them missing the woodwork class as well,' he remembers.

But Larry and his pal Phil Donoghue both got top marks in Irish, English and Maths in their Group Certificate examinations at Granard Vocational school. This gave them the option of going on to study to become teachers of practical subjects.

Learning a Tune the Hard Way

At home, the teenage Larry listened to céilí music on the radio
– Vincent Lowe's band and in particular the Jackie Hearst
Trio. The programmes he would listen to were broadcast for
about 10 minutes before the main news on Radio Éireann
each evening. 'Even though we had no tape recorders back
then we would still pick up bits of tunes and hold on to them
until we would hear them again.' (RTÉ Radio 1 *Irish Music
Legends* – 5 January 2006).

He also shares these memories with Brian Carthy in the
book *The A to Z of Country & Irish Music*. 'My abiding
childhood memory is of a few of us listening to the fill-in
programmes on Radio Éireann so that we could learn to play
a tune properly. As we had no tape recorders we'd each select
a line of the tune and then run out the door so that we
wouldn't confuse each other,' recalls Larry. (*The A to Z of
Country & Irish Music*, p. 41).

Larry still laughs when he thinks back to this slightly less
than scientific way of learning a tune! 'Those were only "filler"
programmes before the main evening news but we loved
listening to them. I remember learning a tune off one of those
broadcasts and continuously playing the first half of it until I
could not forget it. Then I hopped on my bicycle and went
over to my friend's house and played it for him until he had
learned it too. After that we would have to wait until the tune
was played on the radio again to learn the second part of it.'
Larry remembers that only a few céilí bands such as The
Gallowglass or the Richard Fitzgerald Band would have their

records played regularly on these radio shows.

Larry carried on learning tunes on the fiddle until he believed that he had mastered the art of playing the instrument when he was about 18. The Longford man entered his teenage years during the showband decades but he didn't want to be a showband singer or musician at all! However, emigration first, and then immigration, saw him, and a handful of others, become home-grown pop stars who later wooed the Irish for decades at home and abroad. But before he emigrated, apart from going to school and playing music, Larry also played football very successfully. According to broadcaster Paschal Mooney it was football and traditional music that dominated Larry Cunningham's teenage years. 'He played at all grades for his club and with Longford Minors at full back, reaching the Leinster semi-final, where they were beaten by Louth.' (RTÉ Radio 1 *Irish Music Legends* – 5 January 2006).

Long F . . . ing Steps away from the Enemy!

He also became a member of the reserve local defence force known as the LDF. Larry's oldest brother, Michael, was a member and he influenced him to join. Larry recalls that Michael was in the organisation during the World War Two period known as 'the Emergency' in Ireland and he had a medal for his service back then. But while Michael seemed to take his work with the LDF very seriously, Larry was not as enthusiastic. Similar to some other young lads of that generation, it was a great opportunity to take part in some physical training and get free clothes and boots!

'The LDF coat was a mighty garment and the organisation kept half the young lads of the country warm during those winter days and nights. Often when young lads were turning around in their beds all you would hear was the rattling of the buttons on the LDF coat thrown over them! The boots were great too and all of this was a bonus . . . until the time for the annual inspection came around. Then those in the organisation had to have all their uniforms and boots looking resplendent,' laughs Larry.

'My brother made me join and he put me through more drill than a sergeant, just to ensure that I lived up to his expectations. But I was in it just for the fun. Often lads would have to borrow pants and jackets from others when the inspection time came around. Some of us would have ruined the uniforms that we got by using them while digging for potatoes and doing other farm work. On one occasion a top sergeant came from Mullingar to inspect us and of course we were all dressed up to get our stars and stripes,' he remembers. He vividly recalls that year when they had what was billed as a star inspection. If a person got three stars they moved up the ranks to get a stripe. He says getting three stars meant that members qualified to go for two weeks of camp activities in Donegal earning enough wages to last them for six months! Larry and his friends got a laugh when the sergeant came to inspect them. He asked one reservist what steps would he take if he saw the enemy approaching. Larry's colleague replied that he would take 'long 'f . . . ing steps away from the enemy!'

More Money than a Banker or a Teacher

After completing his successful post-primary education at the Vocational School in Granard, Larry took 'long steps away' to Derby in England. Settling into the Irish community there he continued to be involved in his twin loves of football and Irish music. His older brother Eugene had a hotel there at that time. He was also a foreman-scaffolder with Taylor-Woodrow Construction and this influenced Larry's move to Derby.

'I joined the football club straight away and shortly afterwards became a member of a céilí band there, playing the fiddle. We got union wages at that time which was three pounds ten shillings Sterling per night, three nights a week. That was more than any bank manager was earning per week at home and I was getting it for three night's work,' he remembers with a smile.

The young County Longford man was doing well to be earning such high wages as a fledgling fiddle player. But he was entertaining big audiences of fellow emigrants who left Ireland in their thousands in the 1950s. That decade saw the biggest drain of emigrants from the Emerald Isle since Ireland's Great Famine.

In the 1950s, the emigration rate rose to 1.5 per cent of the population, a rate of outflow that was previously surpassed only in the 1840s and 1880s. (*Eire-Ireland: a Journal of Irish Studies.* Mary P. Corcoran. 22 March 2002 – accessmylibary.com)

'I spent two years in England then and I won a senior championship with a team over there. When I came home, instead of going teaching I started in the building trade – and that was in 1958,' adds Larry.

One detects from talking to him today, over 50 years later, that he still has some regrets about not becoming a teacher after returning from exile in England. But if those lingering doubts remain about a possible career as a woodwork teacher, Larry is reticent about elaborating on them. According to him he went to England to 'earn a few pounds' the summer after he finished his studies. 'That time when ten pounds per week was good pay for a teacher I was getting thirty pounds as a carpenter. So I didn't come back for two years,' he says. One suspects that Larry's parents would have preferred if he became a teacher at that time as he says he was 'not very welcome' when he came home. But it seems that his parents accepted that he was going to follow his own path in life anyway and they gave him the space to do so.

The Country 'n' Irish Bono!

The Grafton showband were working around his home area when he returned from England and instead of teaching or joining some religious order, Larry joined them. The young carpenter from Granard was soon to become a big success during the golden era of the Irish showband scene. But fears about giving up his 'day job' resulted in him retiring from music after two years before returning later to become a reluctant star.

Like a dam-burst in a rainstorm, the Ireland of the

swinging 1960s became swamped with showbands. Perhaps the small local bands, among which Larry Cunningham started playing fiddle during the emigration-ravaged 1950s, spawned the big showbands. The first big showband he played with, the Mighty Avons, were previously known as St Bridget's Céilí Band. When Larry fronted the Mighty Avons his success with that band 'started a veritable stampede of Country 'n' Irish artists' – according to a page on the website iangallagher.com. 'Cunningham kick-started the Country 'n' Irish wagon with his UK Top 20 hit "Tribute to Jim Reeves". He became C 'n' I's equivalent of Bono.' That is just one tongue-in-cheek observation on this website which is scathing in many respects about the Country 'n' Irish music scene 'kick-started' by Larry Cunningham.

Larry's music and songs, like those of Hank Williams Junior, were not 'exactly' the same as those of his parents. But there was a strong thread of continuity with the past in the songs he eventually, though reluctantly, sang for showband audiences. Often they were the same tunes and lyrics, albeit arranged differently, that his ancestors had performed beside turf fires in small smoky thatched homes around Leitrim and Longford. His fiddle playing also remained as a small but integral part of the Mighty Avons showband show.

'All during the 10 years that I played with the Mighty Avons I played the fiddle once every night. The late Brian Finlay would sing 'The Banks of the Roses' and I would finish off that part of our show by playing a few jigs. So the tunes that I learned as a child were ones that benefited me during this part of my music career later in life,' says Larry.

Making Old Ballads Cool Again

Unlike some of the 'pop' showband stars of the same era, Larry and the Mighty Avons showband breathed new life into old Irish ballads and, of course, the songs of Jim Reeves. His biggest hit of all, 'Lovely Leitrim', was a precursor for a deluge of other showband (ballad) hits, amid the rock-pop dominated charts of the mid-1960s. Other ballad-boom hits by showbands followed – including some from Sean Dunphy and the Hoedowners, Brendan Bowyer and the Royal, Johnny Kelly and the Capitol and many more. Then along came the hits by the real balladeers including The Dubliners, The Wolfe Tones, Johnny McEvoy, Danny Doyle and later still Christy Moore and Planxty. But of course all of the latter were designated ballad, folk or traditional acts or solo singers. However it was Larry and 'Lovely Leitrim' that seemed to make it acceptable for a showband to perform a ballad and not be booed off the stage!

'Up to then they would throw pennies at you if you were a showband playing a ballad. But "Lovely Leitrim" changed all that and after it was a hit almost every other old Irish ballad around was revived and recorded,' adds Larry. The success of that song all those years ago resulted in longevity for Larry Cunningham on the music scene for over half a century.

But for someone who was a showband legend in his time Larry's home does not display any of the trappings of a showbusiness personality. The home of Larry and Beatrice Cunningham is a neat bungalow only a short distance from where he was born. This home, which he built himself in the early 1960s, is in the next parish to his native one. As he points to a rippling river beside his house, Larry says that one bank of the river is in Abbeylara parish. The other side is in Mullinalaghta, the half parish where he was born. 'It's a bit confusing as the major parish is called Gowna and while Gowna itself is in Cavan, the Mullinalaghta part of the parish is in Longford.'

Today there is no hint of regret in his utterances about not becoming a farmer in his home area, similar to his father. There are no hints of regret either about not carrying on a family tradition by becoming Fr Larry! During his years as a showband star he would share the spotlight and play fundraising football games beside the 'singing priest', the late Fr Michael Cleary. After his death Fr Cleary was discovered to have been a father on the double – a biological father as well as a religious father!

When asked now about not becoming Fr Larry, as his mother might have hoped, Larry quotes something the controversial cleric is supposed to have said.

'As the late Fr Michael Cleary once remarked about being a priest – "it is not a great paying job but it's steady,"' quipped the singer with a smile.

Two
The Old Woman in Black

The elegant old lady dressed in black looked like a character straight out of the TV programme *The Waltons*. Her granddaughter thought so anyway as the butter dripped from the slice of white loaf that she had just toasted over the open fire. The grandmother was serving the young girl toast for breakfast before she cycled to school in Granard. As they listened to the radio, a local lad, Larry Cunningham, sang 'Lovely Leitrim' on the early morning programme. The elegant-looking granny was a fan of Larry long years before her then teenage granddaughter became his wife.

'That's Micky Cunningham's *garsún* (young lad) and he will go far,' said the grandmother as she put the toast on a willow pattern plate for Beatrice Nannery. Having waited for Larry's song to finish it required frantic cycling for two miles to be on time for the first class at St Mary's Convent Secondary School.

At this juncture in his career Larry had moved from the Grafton band to the Mighty Avons and he was on his way to becoming a singing star. Beatrice Nannery was a fan but she was too young yet to go and see him perform at a dance.

Even today Beatrice Cunningham (née Nannery) can, in her mind's eye, picture the scene at her old home in Ballybrine as clear as if it happened yesterday. 'My grandmother was an elegant lady of her time. She wore long clothes and a shawl with a brooch. She never wore a coat and her hair was always styled in a bun on top of her head. She had high boots laced up at the front,' recalls Beatrice.

During her teenage years as an emigrant in the USA, her grandmother, Bridget Lynch, worked for the wealthy Vanderbeck family. Beatrice says she often told great stories about the American family and she was a sweet singer whose favourite song was 'The Rose of Tralee'. According to Beatrice 'on a good day or night' she would 'lift the roof' with her singing of that song and she also loved Larry singing 'Lovely Leitrim'. 'I'll never forget that morning when she spoke about knowing the family of the singer on the radio. My grandmother lived until she was 98 and she followed his career because he was such a local guy,' adds Larry's wife.

A Poor Singer of Pop Songs!

It was years earlier, long before he became a radio star, that Larry had reluctantly joined the Mighty Avons. His decision was based on the assumption that he would be working one night a week and this would not interfere with his day job as a carpenter.

With his previous band, the Grafton, the night work had taken over and that was why he retired from showbusiness after only a short time with them. He was head-hunted by the Grafton after one of their members heard him singing a few comedy songs and playing the fiddle in his local hall. 'I was back home from England and was playing the fiddle and singing a few comedy songs I had written myself,' says Larry. He added that some of the comedy songs were a bit rude but he 'picked the cleanest of them that night' and they went down well with the audience.

'A member of the Grafton asked me afterwards if I would sing with the band. But I told him that I didn't sing, as I did not know any real songs apart from the few comedy ones. I told him that I played the fiddle but doubted if that was what they wanted. However he said that as their own singer was sick they needed a replacement. 'I agreed to join them and said that I would try and learn a few songs from my mother. After joining the band they asked me to learn some of the popular songs of that era. They were the pop songs then. Even though the songs were not that poppish, I didn't like them. I realised that to go anywhere in the business I must be doing songs I liked,' claims Larry.

But while searching for the sort of songs that he would feel comfortable singing, he stayed working with the band and he had the utmost respect for them as musicians.

They said it was ideal if he sang the old ballads that he learned from his mother. Reluctantly Larry decided to do so and he also discovered another type of music that he liked. 'I started out doing the ballads, but believe it or not I thought it was stupid, because I wasn't doing what I wanted to do. However after a few months watching people dancing around to the songs that I was singing, I began to think that perhaps there was something in this after all.'

Cowboy Songs

By this time Larry had developed a liking for what he called 'cowboy songs'. At the time it was known in the United States as country and western music. This type of music influenced Larry after hearing it being performed by a travelling road show at his local hall. 'That time those shows would travel to many of the small rural halls and the one that I first encountered was McCartains Road Show. One performer on this show was dressed up in cowboy gear and he sang those cowboy songs that brought the house down. I wanted to sing those sort of songs but did not know initially where to get them,' Larry recalls.

He had to seek the help of his sister Anna who was married and living in Australia. 'I wrote to her and asked her to try and get me an album of cowboy songs. I remember sending her a half a crown coin (approximately 15 cent) and she sent me an album with a lot of different singers on it. I think every Hank in the business at that time was on it. It had songs by Hank Williams, Hank Thompson, Hank Locklin and many more,' adds Larry.

'I remember selecting Hank Locklin's "Geisha Girl" and two others off the album and learning them. The other two were "Blackboard of My Heart" and "Fraulein". The latter was also a popular Hank Locklin song. The low note to hit was on "Fraulein" and right then I knew that this was the music I wanted to get into,' he adds.

But even though Larry quickly learned these songs the problem for the Grafton musicians was that he had no music for them. 'I had the air and I had learned the words. These boys then had to transpose them and get them ready so that I could sing the songs in the key that suited me. When we put these three songs into our show they were very popular. If we had a record out then it would have been a hit in the area that we were playing in,' says the Granard singer.

Larry and the Grafton built up a loyal following playing the small halls that dotted the countryside of counties Longford, Cavan and Leitrim at that time. It was the era of the emergence of the bigger, barn-style or hay-shed type ballrooms with their 2,000 plus capacity. This new trend would eventually decimate the small rural halls as dancing venues. Even though Larry was to be a big star in the larger ballrooms later on, it was not going to happen for him with the Grafton. The band had five members and sometimes six if it was a bigger dance.

I'll Shoot Kelly Now!

He recalls that the big ballroom near him was The Granada in Granard. But the Grafton weren't big enough yet to get a date there. 'Many big bands were coming there such as The Melody Aces and others. But we were doing fine playing in the small halls in places such as Gowna, Mohill, Drumlish and other venues around our own area. We were attracting crowds of 200 to 300.'

The gable wall is all that's left now.
('My Father's House' by Kevin Sheerin).

The opening lines of that song must have resonance for Larry Cunningham every time he drives through a certain town in the Irish midlands. Even though the song is about a gable wall of a family home, the gable that's significant for Larry is all that's left of one old midlands dancehall. His memories of the hall are humorous ones and they centre on meanness and the difficulty of getting free porter for musicians! The man who operated the hall was considered mean and miserly. He had no ticket checker at the door but did all the work himself. He would lift the hatch at the box office and sell five or six tickets. Then he would unlock the door and let that number of people in before going back to the box office and selling the next five or six tickets. Larry remembers one particular night there with the Grafton band. All the chairs around the walls of the hall were filled with women waiting for the men to arrive from the nearby pub. The band was playing away but nobody was dancing.

A member of the band, who was a fine singer and a brilliant musician, had a speech impediment, not unlike American singing star Mel Tillis. He also had a liking for an odd bottle of porter. 'He asked the bandleader if he could go and get some 'p–p–p–porter' from the owner of the hall before it got too busy. But after another dance or two no porter had arrived at the stage. He shouted across to the bandleader again that if he didn't get porter there'd be trouble. The bandleader still gave him no heed as he felt it would incur the wrath of the promoter to go looking for porter so early during the dance.

· 'I got up and sang my song and then it was the turn of the musician who was waiting for the porter. He started singing "The Wild Colonial Boy". But at the end of the second verse, instead of singing the line "he fired a shot at Kelly" he started singing the same two verses again. He kept doing this for five minutes until the bandleader had to go down to the hall owner and demand the porter. Grudgingly he gave it to him. As the singer saw the porter arriving he turned to the drummer and said, "I'll shoot Kelly now!"'

But as the popularity of the Grafton continued to grow, it also impinged on Larry's day job as a carpenter. He was not happy about this and decided to quit showbusiness before he would become a big star. There was consternation among the fans in the local areas where Larry and the lads were playing. The lads in the band were upset and he says that even some residents in Gowna, where they were based, were upset.

Larry laughs as he recalls the way the fans reacted to him retiring back then. 'It was a bit like somebody leaving Westlife today as far as the local fans were concerned. But while the locals were not happy the band work was starting to take over my life. Actually my mother said it was the best thing to do.

She said I would probably get killed on the road going to work on the mornings after being out playing – as I was driving while half asleep. I thought more of my day job then than I did of working on the music scene at night. Of course I had great comfort after that going to work in the mornings and not being tired after playing the night before. So I was happy with my decision to quit,' he says with a shrug of his shoulders.

The Mighty Avons Come Knocking

But after about six months off the scene he was approached by another new and bigger band with an offer to sing one night a week with them. He had been singing some Jim Reeves' songs before leaving the Grafton band and had got a reputation for hitting the low notes. This is what influenced members of the former St Bridget's Céilí Band, who were changing their name to the Mighty Avons, to seek Larry as a lead singer.

'Two young lads who were probably no more than 17 or 18 years old came to the door at home and asked my mother if there was any chance that I would join the band. Lord rest them both now, they were Gerry Walshe and Brian Finlay. Those wild-eyed young lads said they were members of the Mighty Avons band. When I came home from work my mother told me about their plans. I said I wasn't interested, but a fortnight later they were back again. My mother said I should give them an answer myself one way or another and stop them calling around.'

'So I met them and they told me they had started a new band with eight members. They had no manager but had bookings for one night a week for the following year,' which impressed Larry. 'After playing four or five nights a week with the Grafton I felt that one night a week would not kill me. It meant travelling over to Cavan for rehearsals but I had a little van at that time. We practiced in a hall just outside Cavan in a place called Ballyhaise and they had a great brass section. Basically I only needed to be with the rhythm section for rehearsals and this made it easier as I was still working on the buildings. At the time I was doing all the country songs, which would be one out of every three numbers,' adds Larry.

He was happy enough to be hired as a country singer with the Mighty Avons but he had reservations. He believed some of the band members felt that country music would not be needed for long in the band. 'I wasn't bothered about this, but while I was singing with them I was determined to do it well. My first night with them was in The Embassy Ballroom, Castleblayney on a St Patrick's Night and I feel that at least 2,500 people attended. We were not the reason for such a big crowd. The fact it was St Patrick's Night meant that many people went out dancing. We got 17 pounds for the gig and the other band members met to decide what they would give the new singer,' Larry remembers with a smile.

Even though the band became a co-operative group later on he was not part of the decision-making on the first night – but he was paid two pounds. After some time the band lost one member and manager Charlie McBrien arrived. The late Charlie was from County Tyrone and Larry says he was responsible for getting bigger fees and bigger dates for the band. But even before Charlie came along Larry helped the band move into the bigger ballrooms by getting them a date in The Granada in Granard. It should have been the Grafton band playing for that 'show dance' but when he left the Grafton, Larry asked the promoters, the late Tommy Quinn and Tommy Kiernan, to take the new band instead.

The promoters agreed as they had an impression in their minds that Larry and his new band would sound similar to Larry and the Grafton. That is where they were wrong. The dance was a disaster for Larry and his new band. They were not booked back to The Granada Ballroom for a long time after that, and until their dance programme had changed dramatically. Larry's fans from his Grafton days were at the dance in large numbers but they were unhappy too. Some of them even told Larry after the dance that if he was to continue in the music business he needed a different band as the Mighty Avons were not his style.

Larry is very honest in his views regarding why it all went so wrong on this most important night for his new band. 'Unfortunately when the band saw such a large crowd they lost their heads and everyone was trying to play louder than the musician next to him. I wasn't happy and neither were the dance promoters and we were not asked back there for a long time. We were only allowed back when we had calmed down and our dance programme was different.'

Obviously the young members of the Mighty Avons were on a learning curve. Despite their disaster on the first night in the Granard ballroom they started to attract fans at other venues. They became a huge attraction in Counties Longford, Monaghan, Cavan and Leitrim. For a time, even before any hit record, they were bigger than top national names including The Royal or The Clipper Carlton in those four counties. But Larry admits that until they made the British Pop charts with 'Tribute to Jim Reeves' they meant nothing outside this area. Larry and the lads travelled along the road to stardom at Carnegie Hall, the Royal Albert Hall, the Wembley Arena and countless other venues during their nine years together. They were Paddy Smith (Trumpet), Gerry Walshe (Bass), Brian Finlay (Drums), Peter Smith (Sax and Clarinet), Jimmy Smith (Trombone), Ronnie Griffiths (Keyboards) and Micky Brady (Lead Guitar)

'I remember Micky Brady and his Fender (guitar) coloured blue' states a line in the Declan Nerney hit song 'The Marquee in Drumlish' written decades later by Henry McMahon. Larry became great friends with all the lads but in particular with Micky Brady.

'Micky and myself still do an odd show together and he had great sayings during our days on the road with the Mighty Avons. I remember at one interview being asked how business was going. I quoted something Micky said earlier that day. He said the crowds were so big we hadn't seen floorboards for years,' laughs Larry.

A Cow Chews the Diary

But with success Larry also remembers that costs were rising.

The band had to invest in transport for getting to the gigs.

'Before we got our first big band bus we had two small vans and sometimes we would bring our gear in cars to the gigs. Then we bought a band bus. It was the real deal and we had the name of the band painted on it. Also when you pressed the horn it would play the tune "Colonel Bogey"', quips Larry – as he launches into a bit of lilting to demonstrate what the tune sounds like. It was all a big change from his nights with the Grafton band. Back then sometimes they were all crammed into a car with the boot full of equipment and the bass drum strapped to the roof of the vehicle.

But as time went by, band members, including Larry, often took their own cars to the dance dates. He remembers a time when their road manager, Mick Clerkin, who later launched Daniel O'Donnell, drove a band bus carrying only their equipment! Larry says they were all very excited and enthusiastic at first to be travelling in a band bus but the novelty eventually wore off. Everyone in the band would make their separate way via their own cars to the gigs. These separate travel arrangements could cause confusion regarding where musicians should be on a particular night. The confusion was greater if the band member did not have his diary with him, or if a cow had chewed it, as happened to Larry's diary!

'Most of us in the band, and our manager too, were good enough at football. We would often have games in fields beside marquees before taking to the stage. But sometimes if the game got out of hand some of us might not be on speaking terms when we took to the stage. If we had no goalposts we improvised by using two jackets as makeshift goalposts. One evening we had such a game in a field prior to a marquee dance near Athlone. The game was so intense that it went on late and suddenly we realised that the marquee was half full with dancers. We ran to the back of the stage, put on our band suits as quickly as possible and launched into the dance. The marquee dance was nearly over when I realised that I had left my jacket out in the field where we were playing football earlier. But when I rushed out there I discovered that a cow had eaten part of the jacket. The diary in the inside pocket was half chewed and the pages stuck together with froth from the cow's mouth,' laughs Larry.

The following evening when he was heading off to the next gig he realised that he could not read what was written in the half-chewed diary. Larry thought that they were playing near Ballyhaunis, County Mayo. In an era before the mobile phone he headed for the West.

'I wouldn't normally be the first to arrive at a gig but on that occasion I thought that we had a rehearsal before the dance so I was there early. When I saw the promoter up on a small ladder hanging up a poster for the Mighty Avons I realised that we were there the next week! The promoter looked around and with the shock of seeing me he hit one of his fingers with the hammer instead of hitting the nail to hang the poster.

"Ye f . . . ing so-and-sos are not here until next week," he cried. Quick as a flash I replied that I was just passing through and had only called in for a look. It was then I realised that we were playing in Leitrim village in County Down in Northern

Ireland. When I arrived there the dance was almost over and neither the band nor the crowd were very pleased. But because of that we came back again shortly afterwards and played the same venue and had twice as big a crowd,' he recalls.

The Waitress's Tip

Success with the Mighty Avons resulted in Larry and the lads earning big fees for their dances everywhere from Cricklewood to Chicago and at home from Cork to Donegal. 'Larry Cunningham and the Mighty Avons were the superstars of that time,' claimed Michael Burns of the Galtymore Ballroom, London, in an interview with Paschal Mooney on RTÉ Radio 1 (*Irish Music Legends*, 5 January 2006). The lads in the Mighty Avons were like The Beatles to the teenage girls of that generation according to Beatrice Nannery who was later to marry Larry. 'One girl in my class who was lucky enough to be allowed go to a dance had a beautiful autographed coloured picture of the band,' says Beatrice.

Beatrice couldn't wait to get to a dance at the Granada Ballroom and eventually she was allowed to go and see Muriel Day and the Dave Glover Band there on St Patrick's Night when she was 15. She persuaded her parents to allow her go dancing again on Easter Sunday night and the crowd was even bigger for Larry and the Mighty Avons. Beatrice and her friends danced all night and the words 'send 'em home sweating' were very true she claims. But never in her wildest dreams did she think that the lead singer on stage that night would one day be her husband. 'Definitely not. I remember that when he sang "Lovely Leitrim" there must have been seven or eight rows of people in front of the stage – all just looking up at him. He repeated the song two or three times and the fans just seemed to be in awe of him. To us, Larry and the lads were The Beatles or the U2 of that generation. They were neatly dressed, they wore Pioneer pins and were all decent guys,' she adds.

Amid all the adulation, Larry and the lads were decent with their money too. He gave one tip to a young waitress in a Donegal hotel during the height of his fame that she never forgot. Beatrice Cunningham takes up the story. 'We only heard about this on a trip to Scotland organised recently by Highland Radio. A lot of Donegal people travelled over to Scotland to meet again with family and friends that might have emigrated 40 or 50 years ago. We were staying in a hotel along with the Donegal group. As we were having dinner a mother and daughter were going around the crowded room looking for a seat. I beckoned them to the table where Larry and I were having our meal. It was only when she sat down that she realised she was at the same table as Larry. Then she said something like "Oh my God, we should not be imposing!" but we reassured them that they were most welcome, of course.'

At that stage the woman told them the story from her teenage years. 'She was from Tory Island and every summer as teenagers they would go to Donegal town to work in the hotels there. Her wages were £1 per day. One day when she was serving dinners somebody said Larry Cunningham was in the hotel. As he was a big star then all the girls wanted to serve at his table. She got the task of being waitress at that table and when Larry went up to pay for his meal he handed her a tip of £5. That was the equivalent of her week's wages and she was delighted to get such a generous tip. She went to the local Post Office and opened a savings account. On going back to the island she told her mother about the savings account and how the first £5 was a tip from Larry Cunningham. She never forgot that incident and what a coincidence that over 40 years later she was sitting at a table with us reminiscing about it,' says Beatrice.

Getting a Manager

The sleeve notes on the album 'Larry Cunningham Sings Country and Irish' recall another tale from that era. 'The band arrived at a dancehall in their private cars but nobody had told the road manager that he needed to be there with the band bus containing their instruments! While a fast runner was sent back to collect the bandwagon, Larry and the boys talked to the audience for an hour. The Lord between us and eating turf, if it happened to anyone else they'd have been eaten without salt,' states the writer of the sleeve notes.

Larry also recalls one marquee dance in County Cavan when their drummer disappeared in the middle of a song. 'The stool that the late Brian Finlay was sitting on was at the edge of the stage and it fell off. Brian fell into a heap of pig muck as a sow and her young ones were in the field at the back of the stage. Brian didn't smell well enough to make an immediate comeback on the drums,' laughs Larry.

Even though the Mighty Avons were a co-op band with each member getting approximately the same wage Larry got extra after the success of 'Tribute to Jim Reeves'. As the crowds got bigger things got better and Larry just continued to roll with the flow. But he was always aware that it could end at any time.

The decision to get a manager for the band resulted in Charlie McBrien getting a small office in Cavan. 'Shortly afterwards a girl was appointed as secretary and I said to myself I hope all this works out. There were more expenses but as time went on it became obvious that we needed a manager. Charlie was one of the best but unfortunately he is not with us any more. He may not have been a highly educated man but he was totally committed to his artists. He looked upon me and he sold me as if I was Frank Sinatra! That was the way he saw it and while you were with him he was with you one hundred per cent. He got the top fee for the band, much more than any other manager could get for us at that time. He never drank or smoked and was totally dedicated to the music business.'

It was the lads in the band who hired Charlie as they knew him before Larry did. 'He was gifted with a great memory and if you asked him where we had played on 17 March six years earlier he could tell you without ever checking it up in any diary. He could tell you instantly how many people were at the gig, and how much money we were paid.' Larry's voice lowers and there is a hint of sadness as he remembers his late manager from those days.

Hotel Room Frolics

But laughter coursed through that same voice as he recalled one of the many funny incidents from his days and nights in hotel rooms while touring.

'Three of us were booked into the same room in a hotel in Waterford and while one of the lads was a very clean, methodical person the other fellow was full of mischief. Myself and the mischievous one headed for the room while our neat friend stayed talking to some of the others in the hotel foyer. In the room we discovered an ornamental chamber pot on a shelf beside the window. My colleague took out a banana from his case and after peeling it he broke it into a few sections and placed it in the chamber pot. He then produced a large bottle of red lemonade and poured it in on top of the banana pieces. He then pushed it under one of the beds. When our colleague arrived my mischievous friend asked him if he thought there was a strange smell in the room.' Larry punctuates this story with a few 'F's' that you will not find in the Oxford Dictionary as he recalls what happened next.

'Sure enough this fellow, who saw cleanliness as next to Godliness, searched and found the chamber pot under his bed. He was f . . . ing disgusted and turned a whiter shade of pale. But what happened then was the killer punch. The other fellow took the chamber pot from him and said that perhaps they were wrong about the contents. He dipped his fingers into the red liquid in an apparent bid to take out some of the floating matter, which was now discoloured brown. Our clean colleague ran from the room in horror and got physically sick in the toilet across the hall,' recalls Larry with a laugh.

Leaving the Avons

After more than nine years, nine hit records, countless successful live dances and concerts in Ireland, the UK and the USA, Larry dramatically quit the band. It was a strange move in 1969 just as they seemed to be at the peak of their popularity. He was still with the Mighty Avons when he made his debut at the International Festival of Country Music at the Empire Pool, Wembley in 1969. But behind the scenes the winds of change were blowing and Larry had made up his mind that it was time to move on.

'I told a few of the lads first and they did not react too badly and then I told the others and they disagreed. It came to a point where I had to go anyway. We did not part company all that well but I don't want to talk about that now,' sighs Larry.

The split may have been less than amicable but even now almost 40 years later Larry won't elaborate. Perhaps it is because some of the lads are dead that he does not wish to rake up these old memories of his departure from the Mighty Avons.

'I could see a change coming and a slight drop in attendances. This was not all that remarkable but it was happening. I said to myself that we had worked hard to get to where we were and I felt that for all of us to continue they needed a younger singer and I needed a younger band.'

As the swinging 1960s slipped away Larry left the Mighty

Avons and the 1970s would see him 'walking on new grass' to quote a line from one of his hits. Two years into that decade he married Beatrice Nannery. But her grandmother who cooked the toast for a teenage Beatrice all those years earlier did not live to see this. She died in 1971 but she was aware that Larry was dating Beatrice then. The elegant lady, who looked like a character from *The Waltons* TV show, never knew the details of how Larry's career was kick-started by the 'Tribute to Jim Reeves'. However her granddaughter heard all about it after she became Mrs Larry Cunningham. Micky Cuningham's *garsún* did go far just as the old lady in black had predicted.

But ironically, it was the mood swings of Jim Reeves during his Irish tour that started it all.

Three
Jim Reeves -
You Wrote My Life

The dirty brown spiders scurried for cover in the bowels of the decaying, dusty, dilapidated piano. Shafts of sunlight suddenly lit up their dark abode as the back fell off the broken piano. It was to be used at the performance of Jim Reeves at the floridly named Orchid Ballroom in Lifford, County Donegal – but support singer Larry Cunningham had his doubts. Strings were strained and wires were twisted around each other. It seemed that only spiders, and not ebony and ivory, lived in perfect harmony on the keyboard of this piano! In his mind's eye Larry Cunningham could not see his hero Jim Reeves being happy when his band was presented with this piano to play at the show.

The American star could have sued the promoter, or the spiders, for breach of contract! Jim's widow, Mary Reeves would threaten to sue Larry years later, but not about a broken piano or the 'Tribute to Jim Reeves' hit that launched his career.

It was almost by chance that Larry started listening to the songs of Jim Reeves in the late 1950s. 'A lot of my friends were listening to him and they influenced me.' The song 'He'll Have to Go' (a Reeves' hit in 1959) was the first of Jim's songs that Larry learned.

'It is laughable now when we look back at how we got the words of that song. One of my pals must be the only person in half of Longford to have a tape recorder at the time. It was a poor quality tape recorder but with it we managed to tape the song off the radio. This was not all done at once, as sometimes they would only play part of the song. We would tape that much and eventually we got the final verse on tape as well,' recalls Larry. He admits that he was very proud when he had learned all the lyrics, as very few other singers around his area knew the words of the song at that time.

Larry Cunningham couldn't wait to get to Lifford on that Friday evening of 7 June 1963. Not alone would he see his idol perform, but Larry and the band would share the same stage as 'Gentleman Jim'. He has no idea how they secured the date but he says that 'some stroke was pulled' by somebody and it was a 'lucky stroke' for him and the band.

'We arrived early for rehearsals and the instructions were that the piano be placed on the left-hand side of the stage, as you looked down the hall. We were not using that piano but when we went to move it the back fell off it. Inside it there were as many spiders and cobwebs as you would see in a large, hollowed out, decaying tree trunk in the darkest forest. I said to myself that if the piano player in the Reeves' band got music out of that thing, I would eat my hat,' recalls Larry.

His memories are corroborated by Leo Jackson, a musician with Jim's band, the Blue Boys. He remembered the Lifford piano on an RTÉ Radio programme, *Irish Music Legends,* with presenter Paschal Mooney and in the book *Like a Moth to a Flame.* In the book Leo elaborated on his memories of shattered pianos in many Irish ballrooms during that tour, especially the one in Lifford.

'Half the keys were missing. The white keys were black because the ivory had gone from them. The strings were broken and wrapped around other strings.' (*From a Moth to a Flame* – Rutledge Hill Press 1998, p.190).

On the radio programme Leo explained that the piano was a very important part of the show for the Blue Boys. 'We were a small group with only four pieces. In Jim's contract with this Solomon guy, the promoter, it was agreed that a piano would be there, tuned to A (440). Jim asked Dean Manuel to check the piano and while Dean could get music out of almost anything he could get nothing out of that piano. It was an old upright piano with the back falling off it', said Leo. (*Irish Music Legends* – RTÉ Radio 1 – 5 January 2006).

Jim Reeves Doubles Up

Even though Larry Cunningham did not know beforehand that Jim Reeves was a perfectionist, he still suspected that the broken piano would cause problems.

'I felt that there would be trouble when Reeves and his band arrived. It did not matter to us as our keyboards man, Ronnie Griffiths, used an electric instrument. Ronnie knew that the old piano in the hall was not playable and this led us to suspect that Reeves would not be happy. But we still did not expect him to do what he did to the punters on that night,' says Larry. Jim's reaction to the broken piano included holding the fans responsible for it – almost blaming them. But the American star's sulking was to have a profoundly positive impact on the career path of Larry Cunningham and the Mighty Avons.

There is little doubt about it but Jim Reeves did sulk for much of his Irish tour, as it seems he felt he was being badly treated by promoters. One suspects that his views of Ireland and the Irish remained clouded even when he went back to Nashville. Ray Baker, who was involved in the Jim Reeves' management office in Nashville, still remembers this in 2008.

'I remember him talking about that tour very well. It was in his contract that the promoter had to furnish a piano and it also had to be in perfect pitch, tuned to A (440). He was particular about that as a piano was also a big part of his records. When he arrived at that particular location in Ireland not only was the piano out of tune but also half the strings didn't work. I remember hearing a lot about how unhappy people were after he left the show early. But he was not comfortable singing with an out-of-tune piano. Jim made his likes and dislikes very well known. He would have performed at that hall exquisitely, as he usually did, if the piano was the way it was supposed to be,' said Ray Baker. He made his comments in an interview on Galway Bay FM Radio in December 2008. 'I don't think that Jim ever forgot that incident,' claimed Ray. (*Country Crossroads* – Galway Bay FM, 17 December 2008).

Ray went on to produce many hits for US star Moe Bandy, including 'Hank Williams You Wrote My Life'. This hit suggests that Hank's songs were reflective of Moe's life. In a slightly different context Larry Cunningham could have sang that Jim Reeves had written his life, by paving a path for him on the music scene.

Larry and the Mighty Avons were naive regarding the reasons why Jim and the promoter of his Irish tour were at loggerheads during the Lifford show. The differences were over a raft of issues relating to many aspects of the tour. Poor quality pianos, such as the one in Lifford, were only part of the problem. Jim was asked to play two and sometimes three dates per night, an arrangement unbeknownst to him before his arrival in the Emerald Isle.

In 1963 if a US singer received a contract to play two shows in Donegal, Ireland on 7 June he assumed he was in Donegal. Jim was in Donegal for the two shows, but on arrival he discovered they were 30 miles apart! At 10.30 p.m. he was on stage at The Pavesi Ballroom, Letterkenny. At 12.30 a.m. he was due to sing beside the broken piano at The Orchid Ballroom, Lifford – and suffice to say he was unhappy. 'It was a devilish effort on the part of the promoter to milk Jim's visit to Ireland for everything he possibly could.' The evening line-up of gigs, according to Leo Jackson, were 'nearly impossible to fulfil'. (*From a Moth to a Flame*, p.189).

They Would Have Torn the Place Down

'For a long time afterwards I did not know the full extent of the problems with the promoter who brought him to Ireland,' says Larry.

'Jim did not live up to my expectations in Lifford and I was very disappointed. But later when I found out about the way he was treated by the promoters I felt that perhaps he had a right to be annoyed. However he should not have taken out that annoyance on the punters who paid ten shillings (65 cent today) to see and hear him. He only spent about half an hour or forty-five minutes on stage in Lifford.

'I remember him beckoning to the piano player to check the piano, where I assume the spiders were still hiding. He came out on stage and he had a white towel in his hand, probably to wipe the sweat off himself. The place was packed and when he started to sing it was the same as if his voice was coming from a record. But after doing only shortened versions of his best-known songs he threw the white towel across his shoulder. I did not know it then but this was a signal to his band that he was leaving the stage,' adds Larry.

He recalls that there was a near riot among the crowd of 1,500 or so who wanted to hear much more from the American star. Peter Smith of the Mighty Avons has similar memories. 'He was in very, very bad humour. He said "that goddamn piano is not in tune". He threw a white hankie across his shoulder and pushed a lot of songs into a medley. He never said anything to the people about whether he was going to come back again. He went down to the dressing room, got his coat and disappeared,' stated Peter Smith. (*From a Moth to a Flame,* p.192).

According to this book Peter Smith also remembered that 'angry shouting' filled The Orchid Ballroom and it fell to his bandmate Larry Cunningham to fill the void by doing a musical imitation of Reeves. Larry's memories are similar to those of his colleague Peter Smith.

'Only for the fact that we went on and did a full hour of Jim Reeves' songs there would have been dangerous trouble. They would have torn the place down as fans did at other venues. It was only after we were well into playing our long set of Reeves' songs that they calmed down. What hurt me more afterwards was that he played for an hour and a half at another venue during the tour. He then stood on the running board of his car for ages afterwards signing autographs for the fans. But in my opinion he did not even recognise us as a support band at the Lifford dance. But perhaps he was too upset by the state of the piano and other problems with his tour. In hindsight, his displeasure is understandable,' sighs Larry.

But the Lifford show was only one of many during the Irish tour by Jim Reeves where fans were left disappointed. According to music journalist James Morrissey writing in the book *The Swingin' Sixties,* fans in Kiltimagh, County Mayo, did not hear 'Gentleman Jim' singing at all. The story states that not since Walt Disney had visited the town, at the invitation of a local businessman, had there been such a fuss about a stage or screen personality visiting the town. 'Carloads of couples arrived from all the towns around and how we envied their adult status to have been able to gain admission for ten shillings. As it transpired we were not the only ones to be disappointed. Jim Reeves never performed in Kiltimagh. He claimed the piano was not properly tuned.' (*The Swingin' Sixties* by James Morrissey – Coughlan Publishers 1990, p.54).

The advertisements and posters for the appearances by Jim Reeves and the Blue Boys at venues in Ireland, such as the Donegal shows, state that he was appearing by kind permission of the Irish Federation of Musicians (IFM). 'We were all members of the IFM and an Irish band played on the same stage as Jim at all his gigs here. I remember that there was a survey carried out shortly afterwards and over 600 showbands were members of the federation around that time,' recalls Larry Cunningham. He added that the IFM had no objections to Jim Reeves playing shows here as long as there was also a local group on the bandstand as support act.

In Britain the situation was different. The musicians' union prohibited American musicians from playing concerts unless there were an equal number of British performers playing dates in the States. 'Ireland's union probably opened the country's stages to Jim and the Blue Boys when Jim agreed to include Irish bands on his bills' (*From a Moth to a Flame*, p.188).

A Packet of 'Players' Cigarettes and a Hit!

It was a lucky break for Larry Cunningham and the Mighty Avons that this was the situation in Ireland.

'We were lucky enough that it made our reputation in

Donegal at the time. We were only starting to make headway. We went on and we started playing and Larry started singing the Reeves' songs. We softened the crowd down,' stated Peter Smith. 'Mopping up for Jim was as good as a hit record in Donegal.' (*From a Moth to a Flame*, p.192). But Larry says that the band got no extra money for saving the day (or the night) at the Lifford ballroom. According to him the promoter of the show viewed the part played by the Mighty Avons as good publicity for the band to be on stage with such a big star. He does not remember the fee they were paid either. But as it was a few years after their debut night in Castleblayney where they got £17, he thinks the money in Lifford was 'significantly higher'.

After Jim's Lifford disaster Larry and the band were seen as purveyors of Reeves' songs at dances everywhere. Newspapers reported the next day that the Mighty Avons had saved the day for Jim Reeves. 'That is what started it all for me. It resulted in me getting a name up as a singer if that's what I've got,' suggests Larry modestly.

'The last thing I ever thought of was making a record the night that we played support for Jim Reeves. It was only due to him coming into the equation that the record happened at all. His death came about a year after we worked with him in Lifford and getting to record the tribute song changed my life dramatically,' Larry recalls. It was a strange twist of fate that Jim Reeves died in a plane crash in Tennessee thirteen months after the disastrous Donegal date that launched Larry Cunningham's career. His penchant for performing Reeves' songs and his friendship with a solicitor from Sligo, who wrote songs as a hobby, would soon catapult Cunningham into the British Pop charts.

Eddie Masterson from Tubbercurry, County Sligo was the solicitor and he was making a name for himself in the legal profession in 1964. A colourful character, who usually had a cigarette dangling from his lower lip, he later became known as 'the showband solicitor'. He passed away in Dublin in April 1982. Larry says he first got to know Eddie when he was a solicitor in Carrickmacross, County Monaghan some time before he gave him the words of 'Tribute to Jim Reeves'.

Eddie later moved to Dublin and lived in Barry's Hotel, Great Denmark Street, from where he also operated his practice. 'He was a fan of the Mighty Avons and shortly after the death of Jim he wrote the few verses in tribute to him. He wrote them on the back of a "John Players" cigarette packet. One night he slipped the piece of the cigarette packet containing the words into the pocket of my jacket. He casually said that I should have a look at the words when I would have time. I did so when I went home and was impressed by the way they were put together. I then set out to pick choruses from Jim Reeves' songs that would be relevant to the monologue verses that Eddie had written. They all had to be in slow waltz tempo. Soon afterwards I asked the lads in the rhythm section of our band to rehearse the song with me. I don't think that the brass players were too impressed with it at first. To be honest I didn't know myself if it was a song that would turn out to be good, bad or indifferent,' says Larry.

I Nearly Wet Myself

Ironically it was in Donegal, the county where Jim's show in Lifford was a disaster, that Larry and the lads first discovered that the fans loved the 'Tribute to Jim Reeves' song. He did not even know the words properly the first time he sang it at the Astoria Ballroom in Bundoran.

At that time it was normal for some showband members to take a break from playing at different intervals. While half of the line-up was relaxing the others would keep the show going. Larry says that during these intervals the crowd took very little notice of what was being played. He says you could get away with singing almost anything! Peter Smith's saxophone was standing idle on the centre of the stage. Larry slipped a sheet of paper containing the words of the tribute song under the top key of the instrument. Peter and the other brass players had gone for their break and Larry could sing whatever song he wished.

'The hall was full and many of the dancers were on holidays from Scotland where Jim Reeves' songs were also very popular. I started off singing the song and after the second verse I looked up nervously over the edge of the sheet I had pinned to the sax. When I saw approximately two thousand fans looking up and almost spellbound listening, I nearly wet myself,' says Larry with a laugh. He added that the crowd started shouting to hear the song again and he had to sing it three times. When he started singing it the third time he knew the words 'off by heart'. The boys who played brass were back from their break and Larry and the band knew that they were on to a winner. The rest he says is history, 'music history'.

A few days later Larry and the band went to Pinewood Studios in Bray and recorded 'Tribute to Jim Reeves'. They did all the backing on the recording themselves, no session musicians were booked. They thought it would be easy and a very straightforward recording session. It proved to be the direct opposite. Larry was almost hoarse from all the times that he had to sing the song during that session.

'Back then you could not edit parts out of a song. If anything went wrong while you were recording it you had to do it all over again. I must have sung it at least 50 times. We would be in the middle of it when someone would drop a clanger and we would have to start all over again. Eventually we got it right and it was towards the end of the session that we decided to add piano to it. The woman who owned the studio was a great piano player and when we added her playing to it the mix was complete,' adds Larry.

Larry Almost Kills Relation Over Song on Radio

They brought the finished product to Pye Records, as this company was the biggest label in Ireland at the time. Even though Larry and the lads were confident that Pye would release it, they were in for a shock. A few weeks later they heard the song played on radio but featuring a pop singer with another showband who were contracted to Pye. Larry still steadfastly refuses to name the artist but I understand that he was also a drummer with a pop band. 'He was a good Pop singer but he had no Jim Reeves' note in him. We decided that if this was how Pye Records were treating us we must get another label to release our record quickly.'

According to a story in *Spotlight*, the Irish pop music magazine of December 1964, the band gave the master tape to Cyril Joyce. Larry can't remember the talent spotter's name. But he remembers that he was the Irish agent for the small British-based label, King Records. Larry admits that this man had been interested in getting the song before they gave a copy of the tape to Pye. They knew that King was a small label and they thought the record would have a better chance of success with a bigger company. 'Unfortunately Pye ruled the roost on the recording scene in Ireland at that time,' sighs Larry.

According to the story in *Spotlight*, Cyril Joyce considered this 'Tribute to Jim Reeves' the best of many similar compositions he had heard. Larry says nothing about hearing other Reeves' tribute songs and if they existed they certainly never made any impact. Cyril Joyce sent the tape over to the company's London office. 'It's just a hunch – but I think this might be a winner,' is what he is credited with saying according to the *Spotlight* story. The same story states that it was released in England during the first week of November 1964 and it 'sold over 40,000 copies in the first two weeks alone. Many of the band's fans weren't even aware that they had cut a record until they heard it on Radio Luxembourg and Radio Caroline.' The same story states that it was the least publicised showband disc of the year. 'The publicity came later of course, particularly here at home. Everybody suddenly began to sit up and take notice of a band that had been plodding along unspectacularly for so long.' (*Spotlight* December 1964, p.12).

Silver for Sales of a Quarter of a Million Copies

Larry continues the tale, 'The woman who owned the record label was Mrs Isha King and she was a cousin of the man who was in charge of Radio Caroline (a popular pirate radio ship of the 1960s). Due to her connections in Radio Caroline we got one play per week. It was thanks to this and due to the fact that the record was also put into every jukebox in London that we made the British charts. It was played on Radio Caroline at about seven o'clock every Wednesday evening and very soon our Irish fans also took notice. They would make sure they were listening to the radio at that time no matter what they were at.

'I was working as a builder replacing a flat roof on the home of a relation of mine on one of the first Wednesday evenings that it was played. I could hear the radio from where I was working up on the roof. Once I heard the lines "in Nashville down in Tennessee" I jumped down seven feet off the building. But at the same time the woman of the house was rushing out the back door to tell me I was on the radio. We both collided head-on and I nearly killed the poor woman at the back door of her home,' recalls Larry.

The Longford singer says the pace of life was very different in rural Ireland during those times. To be heard singing on the radio signified to many of the older people that the singer was away in some studio singing live. 'I remember one of my neighbours walking past a house where I was repairing a roof one morning and we chatted for a while. When he got home a few minutes later his wife told him that he had just missed hearing Larry Cunningham singing on the radio. "You're a liar," said the man, "he could not be away singing on the radio as I was talking to him five minutes ago down the road,"' laughs Larry.

Another Larry, RTÉ broadcaster Larry Gogan, also laughs as he proudly remembers his friend Larry Cunningham being in the British Pop charts. 'It was phenomenal at that time. To make the Irish charts was great but being in the British charts was brilliant. There was no jumping around for Larry even though he was in there among all those rock stars. He was so laid-back; if he was any more laid-back he would fall off his stool. Larry was just a smooth country singer in the Jim Reeves' style. He just let his smooth voice carry the song and it was a sensation at the time.' (*Irish Music Legends* RTÉ Radio 1 – 5 January 2006).

Amid the nostalgia after the death of Jim, Larry's tribute song edged closer to the Top 20 in the UK. He got the chance to push it further up the charts with an appearance on the TV show *Top of the Pops*. Larry says that at the time he did not understand the real significance of being on a pop charts TV show in Britain. All he remembers is that top pop DJ of that era, Jimmy Saville, was the presenter and Larry says he sang to a backing track. The only other artist that he remembers from that TV show was Cliff Richard. 'Can you imagine me doing a monologue on *Top of the Pops*? I suppose I had a hard neck then and I still have one. Looking back it seems crazy to perform a monologue on a British TV show featuring rock singers.'

Larry's song was bubbling under the Top 30. It was tipped for the top after his TV appearance and he says it moved up to Number 28. But afterwards it fell away and he feels that if it had been released on a bigger label it would have gone much higher. 'I wanted someone to keep plugging it on the radio programmes in England. If that was done it could even have gone all the way to Number One. I'm not saying so just because I was singing it. But in people's minds Jim Reeves was still a man alive.'

Sales of the song were phenomenal and Larry and the Mighty Avons were guests of honour at a very memorable function in a London hotel in early 1965. He was presented with a silver disc for worldwide sales in excess of 250,000 copies of 'Tribute to Jim Reeves'. 'I knew the sales were big from the amount of people who would bring the record to the dances to have it autographed. This was only one section of the record-buying public. Even judging by the number of dancers that had the disc we knew it was a big seller. But we were amazed at the final figure,' he claims.

Living on the Back of a Dead Man!

Strange as it may seem it was to be over six years later before Larry would travel to Nashville to record a full album of Reeves' songs. This was titled 'Larry Cunningham Remembers

Jim Reeves'. During those recording sessions in Monument Studios he also re-recorded the 'Tribute to Jim Reeves' with some members of Elvis Presley's backing band. This version of the song has been re-released in recent times on Larry's double CD *Real Country Music* on the Ceol label. So almost 45 years after it was first recorded Larry's 'Tribute To Jim Reeves' is again available on disc. Copies of the 1964 hit single can still be purchased from record collectors on the Internet. There is even a version of Larry's song on YouTube, which is coupled with black and white footage of Jim Reeves in concert. Recent comments posted on this internet site show that people in the UK are still reminiscing about Larry's song. This is amazing longevity for any tribute song.

However back in the mid 1960s the success did not continue to the same extent with the next two singles that Larry released after his tribute hit. Even though they were both Jim Reeves' songs they failed to make any impact on the British charts. 'The interest started to fall off and magazines such as *Spotlight* were suggesting that I was making my career on the back of a dead man,' recalls Larry. Strange as it may seem the 'B' side of his 'Tribute to Jim Reeves' is now a song that Larry is often requested to sing at funerals. It is the Reeves' song 'Take My Hand, Precious Lord'. According to the initial review in *Spotlight* magazine, Larry's treatment of this song was 'practically indistinguishable from Reeves' own version of the same number'. (*Spotlight* December 1964, p.12)

But Larry Cunningham insists that nobody could sound as good as Jim Reeves and he is adamant that it is only by chance that he sounds somewhat similar. 'There is no night, since

1964, that I go on stage without doing a small tribute featuring some Jim Reeves' songs, but it is in my own style. Of course I'm happy if people think that there are similarities in our voices, I am honoured if they do so. But all I do is sing the songs that he recorded because no one else can ever sing them the way that he did. He was the original and the best.'

Reeves' Widow Threatens to Sue Larry

Larry feels that a golden opportunity was lost for theatre tours in the UK at the time of the success of the Jim Reeves' tribute song. He claims that if some promoter had hired major concerts venues, including The Royal Albert Hall, the fans would have come in their thousands to hear the tribute song.

'We had enough Jim Reeves' songs to do at least an hour and a half of a concert programme. If management targeted the theatre scene then it could have opened up a whole new touring circuit for us. This would be separate from the Irish ballrooms in the UK where we were doing well anyway.'

Many years later Larry Cunningham was to make an impression on the British Concert and Country scene via the Wembley Festivals. Beatrice Cunningham recalls a strange encounter there with Jim's widow, Mary Reeves, at a time when she was threatening to sue Larry.

The widow of the American star was at the Wembley Country Festival and she admired the engagement ring worn by Larry Cunningham's bride-to-be.

'Larry was appearing at the Wembley Festival that year and

it was a great occasion for us to travel over and have an enjoyable weekend in London. Mary Reeves had an exhibition stand at the arena where she was selling some of Jim's records and books. She was there signing autographs and her second husband was with her at the stand,' recalls Beatrice. To this day she treasures a photograph of Jim's widow and her second husband, Terry Davis. It was autographed for her by Mary Reeves.

'I was in the queue waiting for her autograph when she spotted the engagement ring on my finger. She took my hand and said "Oh! What a beautiful ring!" She did not know who I was but it suddenly dawned on me that she was threatening to sue my husband-to-be over another matter. In the back of my mind I was thinking that if she knew who gave me the ring she might not be so friendly.

'At the time Mary and her management were threatening to sue Larry because he had named his new band the Blue Boys. This was the same name as the band that toured with Jim Reeves. But Larry and his management quickly changed the name to the Country Blue Boys and it ended at that,' she adds.

Beatrice and Larry Cunningham say the brightly-coloured autographed printed card of Mary Reeves and her second husband may be a collector's item. On the reverse side it is autographed in neat handwriting. The three words written in faded brown felt pen ink simply state 'Thanks. Mary Reeves'. In the photo, directly behind the heads of Mary and her husband, some colourful abstract art images are visible beside a dark wooden fireplace. The wood possibly looks similar to, but perhaps less dusty than, the dark wood on the dilapidated piano all those years earlier in The Orchid Ballroom, Lifford. A star-shaped, brightly-coloured abstract art image beside the dark wooden fireplace stands out from the others. One could imagine that it is an abstract art image of a seven-legged spider! But if so, it is orange-coloured and not dirty dark brown like the insects that scurried into the bowels of the broken piano in The Orchid ballroom. Those spiders sent Jim Reeves and his band scurrying out of town in search of unbroken pianos in other halls. But perhaps they saved the day for Larry Cunningham and helped launch him on the road to stardom.

Spiders are said to be lucky!

Four
If I Were a Carpenter

If I were a carpenter
And you were a lady
Would you marry me anyway?
Would you have my baby?

– James Timothy Hardin

Johnny Cash and June Carter were at No 2 in the US Country charts in the spring of 1970 with 'If I were a Carpenter'. Around this time Longford's singing carpenter, Larry Cunningham, may have pondered quoting the first four lines of that hit song when courting his young lover! When Beatrice became his bride in 1972 he thought he could leave the singing scene and go back to being a carpenter. But how wrong those thoughts turned out to be.

As the showbusiness courtship, wedding and honeymoon went ahead, few knew of a hair-raising medical problem facing

Larry. Perhaps his hectic schedule as a singing star and his success as a builder and businessman contributed to the medical problem. Less than four years earlier, on 30 September 1968, Larry opened his supermarket in Granard. The date might not have seemed significant to him. But it was the 30th anniversary of British Prime Minister Neville Chamberlain returning from a meeting with Adolf Hitler and waving an agreement in the air declaring 'peace in our time'. How wrong his thoughts also turned out to be!

Like a lot of other Longford carpenters of his age Larry Cunningham had progressed from being a carpenter to becoming a fully-fledged builder by 1968. Then he became a supermarket developer and owner. All this building and business success started when he constructed his own home. But the pressures of success may also have resulted in Larry requiring painful medical treatment in the USA during his honeymoon.

The House that Larry Built

'Back in 1960 I did most of the work building the house that we still live in today. Carpentry was my trade but in those days you did everything. You plastered, slated the roof and did everything else. The house is 49 years old now and it is only last year that we had to replace the wood facade. After all those years it is still standing so I must have done something right,' he claims.

Larry built his family home during the early days when he

was singing with the Mighty Avons and he says it is only one of several houses that he built. 'I built dozens of houses after that. Often I would rush home to wash the splatters of concrete off myself at six or seven in the evening. Then it was off to play with the band somewhere around the country.'

He had four or five men working with him building the houses during those times. He might be playing at some dancehall or carnival marquee until 2 a.m. and perhaps signing autographs and chatting to fans for a further hour. But Larry would still be on the building site a few hours later. 'I would be on the site at about 10 a.m., but on arrival I would often be in terrible bad form. However, after about an hour up on the roof with the fresh air going into the lungs the form would improve. The work would give you a great appetite,' adds Larry. 'You would eat like a horse out on the building site but if you stayed at home you would have no appetite at all.'

Years later when interviewed by Shay Healy for an RTÉ TV programme Larry says those days working on roofs may have helped his health too. On the TV show *Little Bit Country* Shay Healy asked Larry about a series of heart operations he had in the year 2000. 'The doctors told me that while my singing colleagues were in bed in the mornings I was on roofs and this may have saved my life,' said Larry. (*Little Bit Country* RTÉ 1 29 October 2006).

On the same TV show he said he never went to a dance without having the toolbox for his carpentry work in the boot of his car. That TV programme also showed footage of a young Larry Cunningham from an earlier TV show. He is singing, albeit with very little feeling, The Beatles' hit 'A Hard Day's

Night', as part of an Irish quartet. Larry has concrete memories of that TV appearance!

'I remember it was on the RTÉ programme *Smash Hits*. Those appearing were Dickie Rock, Brendan Bowyer, Joe McCarthy of The Dixies and myself. Going up to Dublin for the show, I didn't even know where the RTÉ studios were. It was all a rush as I was working with concrete on a building site until a short time before I left home.' As the make-up artist was putting the finishing touches to Larry to get him ready to face the cameras she encountered a strange problem. 'She discovered that I had splatters of concrete on my eyelids. She had to apply some sort of solution to take it off before she could put on the make-up. If the other singers knew that they would have a good laugh.'

While most other singers were concentrating on their music careers only, Larry continued to work as a carpenter and builder. He purchased an almost derelict property on the main street of Granard and developed it into a supermarket.

'I renovated the building after buying it and when we opened it as a supermarket many people said it wouldn't work.' But it did work and people in this Longford town in the late 1960s embraced this self-service shopping experience. Little did Larry know that employing a young lady, Beatrice Nannery, as a secretary meant he was also embracing a life-changing experience.

It Wasn't Love at First Sight

'I needed a secretary as I had opened a supermarket and it was vital to have somebody to deal with all the paperwork. We advertised the position and I went out to the home of one of the applicants to meet her. There is no question about it but it was the best meeting I ever had,' recalls Larry.

Beatrice Nannery laughs when asked if her initial meeting with Larry Cunningham was love at first sight. 'Certainly not, I was young and carefree then. All that was on my mind, and the minds of my friends, was to get to dances and enjoy ourselves. Knowing Larry was a great advantage and when he was playing within a 20- or 25-mile radius we were sure of getting a lift. We were all fans of country music and of him and many of the other showbands. For the first year that I worked with Larry it certainly was business only. Then I was put in charge of the fan club and at Christmas time we would post to the members calendars, records or some other piece of memorabilia. We would mail thousands of packages to all those in his fan club at that time.'

The teenage Beatric Nannery got a glimpse of the feelings of many of Larry's female fans who would write to the fan club. She smiles as she reminisces. 'The letters came in from all those adoring fans who loved him. He would reply to many of their queries and I would look after sending back the replies. Sometimes they might want an autographed picture for themselves or for somebody else. I also dealt with the renewal of membership and all that was associated with that,' she recalls.

In 1970 Larry diversified further in his business life and he opened a dry cleaning business beside the supermarket in Granard. This required more staff and for Beatrice Nannery it obviously meant more work regarding wages, receipts and keeping tabs on all payments. At one stage they had nine collection points for clothes for dry cleaning around Longford and surrounding counties. 'I had to learn how to operate the dry cleaning equipment myself and how to repair the machines if they broke down,' adds Larry. He also had an annual dinner dance for his enterprises and staff at this time and it was also a big social occasion in Granard.

In the midst of all this increasing workload, romance started for the teenage secretary and her singing boss. But Beatrice can't pinpoint the exact moment or date when this happened. 'I don't know how or when we actually started going out together. But I remember that we started travelling to different events together around the country. We went to Ennis once to a dance and to me at that time it was a huge distance to travel.' Sometime after Larry opened his supermarket, and around the time he was leaving the Mighty Avons, romance blossomed between him and Beatrice.

'It was very low profile at first as Larry was on the road up to six nights a week. He would also be doing some charity concerts on Monday nights. Going to those charity concerts might be our only night out together as he was usually on his own,' reflects Beatrice. Larry says that people got to know that he had a steady girlfriend and the way the female fans reacted did not bother him.

'My intention was that the day I would get married I would

quit the music. I intended to go back to the building business but that plan lasted less than 12 months. I had to go back singing and I haven't really stopped since.' In an article in *The Longford Leader* newspaper in 1987 Eddie Coffey refers to Larry's short retirement after his marriage. 'He fulfilled his promise for a short while – just over six months in fact. In that time he built two houses, one of which was for Fr Egan in Abbeylara.' (*The Longford Leader,* 19 June 1987)

Planned Confusion about Engagement

Beatrice admits that even before they got engaged, being in love with Larry posed its own problems. Those included work constraints and the fact that he was so much in the public eye.

'I was working with my colleagues in his business and he was away performing. He was high profile and I was low profile. But I was just busy at work. I was young and strangely enough we were able to cope.' However one gets the impression that it was not all sweetness and light and Beatrice might have had to cope with the barbed comments of others about her romance.

'A lot of the stuff said to me could be hurtful, but I just accepted it and got on with life. I remember saying to Larry that he was a bit older than me and while I would be faithful it was up to him to do what he wanted to do. We made a go of our relationship because both of us accepted what our lives and work demanded. He had to go out and share his life with his fans. I was happy to see him do that because I trusted him.

We trusted each other even though there were many days and weeks when we were apart.'

Beatrice and Larry got engaged on her 21st birthday, which was on 20 August 1971. But it was nine weeks later before the general public knew of the engagement. 'We were engaged in Dublin and shortly afterwards Larry was going on a three weeks tour of England. Immediately after that he was off on a six weeks tour of the USA. We agreed that as I would be nine weeks on my own I would not wear the engagement ring until he was home towards the end of October,' Beatrice recalls.

Due to Larry's high profile and that fact that many of their friends knew they were going to Dublin for Beatrice's 21st they had to camouflage their engagement. 'Some people were expecting to see me with a ring on our return. But Larry also bought me a beautiful suede coat while we were in Dublin. This confused those who were waiting to see the ring. The new coat was seen by many as his gift for my 21st birthday. I locked the engagement ring in one of the little drawers in the safe in the office of the shop. Occasionally when no one was around I would take out the ring. I would have a look at it and smile,' recalls Beatrice as she twists the beautiful sparkling ring still on her finger today.

Larry sits silently and uneasily bashful by her side as his wife tells all this. She also speaks about the love letters he sent her while he was away on tour in America during the first weeks of their 'secret' engagement. 'He wrote me some nice letters. It was difficult to make phone contact back then. Different parts of America have different time zones. When he was touring over on the west coast we might have to deal with a 10-hour time difference.'

'He arrived back around 22 October. We went off again to Dublin on the following day and I came back that evening wearing the ring and we told my parents. When I told my mother we were getting married in February all that was worrying her was that the weather might be cold and miserable then,' she remembers.

Showbusiness Wedding Hides a Hair-Raising Health Worry

Larry had one cloud over his head that was more major than the weather when he and Beatrice got married on 9 February 1972. 'It was the most beautiful weather. There wasn't a cloud in the sky, so somebody must have been praying for us,' suggests Beatrice. But there were clouds of worry at the back of Larry's head. A medical problem that manifested itself only months before the wedding would manifest itself more in America during the honeymoon. However for anyone looking at the photographs in the press their showbusiness wedding was one where no clouds of any type were visible. During their honeymoon the medical cloud that hung over Larry's head was to end up having a silver lining!

On their wedding day Beatrice's brother was the priest in charge of the ceremony. He is Monsignor Bart Nannery who is now Dean of the Catholic Cathedral in Plymouth City. They were married in St Bernard's Church, Abbeylara and over 450 guests attended. The wedding reception was in the Nuremore Hotel, Carrickmacross, County Monaghan as it was the only hotel in the area big enough to cater for the crowd.

The media descended on the church and the hotel for the event. The local post office got the brunt of the calls in advance of the wedding according to Beatrice. 'We had no phone at my home. So all the calls would come to the post office in my home village of Kilcogy, County Cavan. Someone would come to our house from the post office to say that *The Irish Press* or the *Irish Independent* or some other newspaper were looking for details. I stayed well away – making no comments as I had too much to do in making the wedding arrangements.'

When Beatrice the bride arrived at the church she discovered that there were as many people outside as inside and this came as a shock to her. 'The place was crowded with people and when the musicians started to play "The Wedding March" I began to cry. What made me cry was that everybody in the church turned in my direction and cameras were flashing all around me. I got overcome by all of this. When we got to the altar I remember my brother being there which was a great consolation for me. The parish priest Fr Michael Egan caught me by the arm and said that everything would be fine and this calmed me,' she adds. Larry says he sang at their wedding reception, as did many of his contemporaries from the Irish showbusiness scene. Beatrice says that she believes the wedding reception went on for 'about three days' but she and Larry had to head for Dublin to catch a flight to the USA the next morning.

Despite being in all the daily newspapers Beatrice had to go to the American Embassy that morning for her passport and to prove she was Beatrice Cunningham. 'We had to be there at 8 a.m. and our flight was leaving at 9.30 a.m. We got delayed in traffic and when we arrived at Dublin Airport the plane was ready to go and we were the last two passengers. In fact they delayed the flight for us. On the plane were Earl Gill and the Hoedowners Showband and as soon as we boarded they started singing "Congratulations". Suddenly I realised that this was going to be the start of a different life for me as everyone knew who we were,' she recalls.

Medical Problem Worsens During Honeymoon

The newly-weds flew to New York and then on to Florida. Here they discovered that Larry's medical worries were worse had they had thought. As a result of this they had to cut short their honeymoon and return to New York. It was only after the wedding that Larry and Beatrice revealed to their close family and friends a strange medical trauma he endured coming up to the big event. The first signs of this medical problem emerged shortly before Christmas 1971.

Larry went to his local barber for a haircut and it was discovered that he had bald spots at the back of his scalp. He seemed set to lose all his hair and this was a worry before the wedding and afterwards during the honeymoon. Pressure of work and countless other factors were said to be the cause. Before the wedding Larry went to some of the top specialists both in Ireland and in the UK while he was on tour there.

He was told by an associate in the music business in Britain that he had solved a similar problem by having a six-months' rest in the Bahamas. But due to the wedding and a punishing work schedule Larry knew that taking six months off anywhere was not on for him. A doctor in Longford told him that what he was suffering from was *alopecia*. But it might be possible to solve the problem with new medical treatment available only in America at that time. The painful treatment was said to be successful for many patients. As Larry was going to be on tour in the USA, while also on his honeymoon, plans were made for his medical treatment there as well. A deterioration in his condition during the early days of the honeymoon required that the newly-weds return from Florida to New York.

'Larry would be washing his hair and so much of it was falling out that it would be blocking the sink. We came back to New York early and met his sister there. Another great friend of his, Br Oliver Sheridan, was there and he had helped organise that he go to a specialist,' says Beatrice. Larry has vivid memories of the worry and the painful treatment he endured for his hair loss. 'Much of the hair on the back of my head was nearly gone when I went to this Dr Ferguson in New York. I got nine injections between the scalp and the skull and I must have slept for a solid two days afterwards.'

According to Beatrice they took him back to his sister's home in Bayside, New York, where they had difficulty getting him to wake up. She said he slept so long they thought he was never going to awaken. As soon as he did he had to head off on tour of venues all over the States. 'After nine days I had to be back in that doctor's surgery in New York for more injections,' adds Larry. Beatrice Cunningham says she then accompanied her husband on tour for a few nights but after that she had to fly home. He continued his tour but they both had to contend with the uncertainty of not knowing what the outcome of his medical treatment would be.

After his third visit to the New York medical specialist the hair started to grow back on Larry's bald patches. But it grew back as grey hair. He had to dye these grey patches for a few months. But after that the colour returned to normal. Larry says that thankfully he never had problems with *alopecia* since then.

'Of course the cloud that lifted off my head had a silver lining. All my hair's changed to silver since then,' laughs Larry.

The Arrival of the Stork

In the rural Ireland where Larry and Beatrice grew up, children were often told that babies were brought by the stork or found under cabbage leaves! As the post-modernity era of the 1970s unfurled its flag, emblazoned with myriad images of permissiveness and pluralism, the rural childbearing stork lost its relevance. But in a lighter moment another stork held sway at Cunningham's supermarket.

Memories of the supermarket stork still cause Beatrice and Larry to emit loud guffaws of laughter. Apart from their light-hearted encounter with the supermarket stork the other stork visited Larry and Beatrice as their four bouncing babies were born. Their first child, Regina, was born in Mount Carmel Hospital, Dublin on Tuesday 2 April 1973. As she came into the world Larry was singing on stage at a dance in The Olympic Ballroom. Beatrice has vivid memories of this momentous occasion. 'It was a Doctor Strong who delivered her. I recall that when she was born he said she was the most beautiful child he had ever seen. The doctor asked me if they called Larry "the king". When I replied this was true he said something like "this is a beautiful princess fit for a king." I was in so much pain that I don't think I carried on the conversation with him,' she adds.

When their second baby, Sinéad, came along, Beatrice says she was delighted that it was a girl. She did not have a sister and she was pleased that little Regina now had one. She was born in June 1975 and Larry was on stage that night too. He was playing in Bundoran and when he got home at 6 a.m. he went to drive Beatrice to the same Dublin hospital where Regina was born. But they only got six miles – as far as The Manor Nursing Home in Edgeworthstown. The local GP said he would ring The Manor and ask them to take Beatrice in there to see how she was doing en route to Dublin. But events unfolded quickly and Sinéad was born on a trolley in the lift there.

A few years passed before Lorcán was born and this time Larry again rushed home from a dance date and arrived in the nick of time. 'He was home at about 7.30 a.m. I remember that we had men working on an extension to the house and I said I needed to go before they arrived. We headed for Mullingar and at this stage everybody was ringing the hospital to know if our baby was born. So I told Larry not to appear at the hospital at all. He would only attract attention and what people did not know would not bother them. He dropped me at the door with my bag and I headed in on my own. I told him not to call me until 2 o'clock that afternoon and as the clock was striking 2 in the labour ward Lorchan was born,' she adds. Beatrice says this was another very exciting event as he was their first son and Larry's mother was also delighted that he had an heir.

Three years later when Barry was born Larry was again away on stage in Drumcong, County Leitrim. 'That was a long slow labour for about 12 hours and I thought having that baby was going to be the end of me,' admits Beatrice. For a while after getting married she had juggled home life as a mother with that of working in the supermarket. But she decided that it was important to be with the children as they were growing up and she became a full-time mother. However both she and Larry encountered the supermarket stork first. A transport dispute disrupted the distribution of goods from a factory in Louth, which caused this stork to fly north only, according to Larry.

Customers in shops in the South, including those at Cunningham's supermarket, could no longer get the popular 'Stork' margarine. But Larry headed North after the 'Stork' as the margarine was still on sale in the Six Counties. He loaded a van 'to the roof' with boxes of the product. Larry criss-crossed the border via unapproved roads to avoid the Customs Officers seizing the goods. Now he could again stock his shop shelves with Stork and keep the customers happy. It was only then he noticed that the packages of Stork margarine sold in the North had the Queen's head emblazoned on the back.

As they watched a local Garda sergeant examining the packages on the shelves Larry and Beatrice thought they were in trouble. But the long arm of the law filled his basket with slabs of Stork margarine. The sergeant remarked to Larry that as it was the only shop where he could buy Stork he was stocking up to 'keep the pan busy'. Larry then told him he feared the worse when he saw him looking at the Queen's head on the back of packets.

'I need the Stork for frying and I don't care if it's the Queen's backside that's pictured on it,' was the sergeant's slightly crude reply.

Never Together for Christmas Dinners

On a more serious note, Beatrice says the four children the stork brought them were all healthy and happy. She often counted her blessings when she saw others at places where Larry played fund-raising dances.

'I remember going to one place with him where all the children were in wheelchairs and I said I would never complain about anything again,' recalls Beatrice. She added that these experiences changed her attitude regarding the fact that the only night he was off they could not go out together. This was due to his charity work. 'Larry's charity work on Monday nights might be to raise funds for mentally or physically retarded children or to help re-roof a church or school. It didn't matter if it was anywhere from Cork to Donegal, Larry gave his Monday nights free for charity,' recalls his wife.

'Another problem in these years was that Larry would never have Christmas dinner with us. He would be away entertaining in the local hospitals on Christmas Day. A few times I went with him and we would meet people of all ages who were there due to different illnesses. You always felt better coming home realising that the bit of entertainment Larry did helped brighten their lives. We could cook Christmas dinner any time and after all it is only another meal. We became supportive of the charity work that he was doing, even on Christmas Days. At one time I joked with him that we could nearly paper a wall in the house with Helen Steiner Rice 'Thank You' cards from all those charities. But he did this work with a heart and a half. My attitude was that one 'Hail Mary' from those that he helped would also help bring us through life,' she adds.

While Beatrice stayed in the background for most of the first 25 years of their married life she was conscious that as the children got older they would get some flack from their peers at school about having a famous father. But they were all able to deal with it in their own ways. 'They were all good children. They have done very well and they have given us great enjoyment in life,' she says.

Married or Single for the Fans?

Larry says that he never worried about the female fans disappearing when he was a married singer with a young family. 'I don't think that in my lifetime any of the bands I was in ever sent out the sort of message that all we wanted was female fans. I never looked upon myself as being a star but I was simply singing something I liked to sing. I considered myself very lucky to have a following who liked that sort of material. It didn't matter a damn to them if I was married or single. Over 30 years later I think I have proved that was right as many of them still come to our shows,' he claims.

Larry is adamant that being upfront and not hiding from his fans that he was a married man was a good decision and one that he never regretted. 'Unfortunately I watched the opposite happening when some stars tried to hide this. Perhaps I was lucky enough that I took note of the damage this hiding of the truth did to a few other singers before I was married. They thought that later on when they were bigger stars they could then tell the truth. But unfortunately when they told the truth that they were married many of their fans dropped them to the lower end of the scale.'

When it is pointed out that it must still be hard for showbusinesss marriages to survive, Beatrice admits that this question is a 'tough one'. 'I suppose the first main ingredient in any marriage is trust. I had to have the trust in him because I was the one that was at home. But it was easier for me as he was the one that was in the limelight all the time. Then of course we were both so busy that I think this helped too. My father often said that if a person minds the business within his or her own four walls one has lots to do. How right he was with this saying,' she concludes. Larry and Beatrice agree that family values passed down to them by their parents were invaluable to them in raising their own children and now in enjoying their grandchildren. In their own quiet way it is very obvious that Larry and Beatrice are adoring grandparents.

The cauldron of life containing showbusiness marriages never seems to have caused their relationship to boil over or burn out. Despite Larry's public profile there seems to have existed a certain stability in their home which may have counteracted the pressures from outside sources.

Even though the crowds were getting bigger all the time Larry never gave up the 'day job' as a builder. It is amazing that he was able to continue on and do his carpentry work even after having massive hits. While away on tours abroad for three or four weeks at a time the men who worked on his building projects carried on. On occasions too the band members had to carry on without him, particularly at rehearsals if some building project needed completion. The sleeve notes on the album 'Larry Cunningham sings Country and Irish with the Mighty Avons' confirms his absence from rehearsals. The writer was told by bandleader Jimmy Smith that Larry was often missing in action!

'To tell you the truth I haven't seen him for three days. He's out in the country selling haybarns,' said Jimmy. Around the time of Jimmy's remarks Larry was building a large block of flats on property beside his new supermarket. At that time there was big demand from people renting flats in Granard.

'We had Gardaí, teachers, factory workers and many others living in those flats. We had many a good music session there too and a lot of happy memories from those times,' he says.

His memories of the supermarket business are good ones too. But the times keep changing and when Larry left the supermarket scene he changed the building into a leisure centre. 'We had all the facilities there – steamrooms, saunas, treadmills and all that. But later still I worked on refurbishing the building for a third time when we reconstructed it to make it suitable as a Youthreach facility for the Vocational Education Committee,' adds Larry.

Does this famous 'singing chippie' from Longford do any carpentry now that he is in his 70s? Larry replied in the affirmative. 'Yes, but now it is usually jobs for family members and friends. Of course I still have to do the odd carpentry job for Beatrice around the house,' says the singing carpenter as he smiles at his still vivacious wife. He is still a carpenter and she is still his lady who married him anyway and they have their babies. For them the lyrics of the Johnny Cash – June Carter hit song must still reverberate with reminiscences of their courtship back in 1970.

If I worked my hands in wood
Would you still love me?
I'd answer you yes I would
Would you not be above me?

If you were a carpenter
And I was a lady
I'd marry you anyway
I'd have your baby. — James Timothy Hardin

Five

Bloody End for 'Lovely Leitrim' Man

T he love of liberty seems destined to have meant a bloody death, either at home or in the 'land of liberty' for the 'Lovely Leitrim' man. If slimy slugs crawled over his stomach as he trained among the wet wild willows and green rushes near Selton Hill, they were harmless. Not so the fatal slugs that tore into his stomach later on far from the friendly fields of 'Lovely Leitrim', which inspired his song. Six of his young comrades, who trained also to fight for freedom perhaps among the wet green rushes and willows, died in a bloodbath on Selton Hill. The foreign slugs from brutal Black and Tan guns that shot his six friends spawned an almost unknown verse for his song 'Lovely Leitrim'. However that same verse and another by chance failed to make the final cut for Larry Cunningham's hit record.

'At the time Radio Éireann was Ireland's only station. As the powers there were unlikely to play any record that was over 2 minutes 50 seconds we had to cut two verses,' Larry explains. By eliminating two verses it was possible to trim the song to 2 minutes and 45 seconds, which was the cut that helped make it more radio friendly. Even though the Selton Hill verse fell on the cutting-room floor, Sheemore Hill, the scene of another famous bloody battle, did get a mention. But irrespective of what changes were made to the 'Lovely Leitrim' man's song it was destined for greatness as he was also.

While he may never have envisaged its huge hit potential he seems to have had a premonition of his own bloody death. Another almost unknown poem from his pen alludes to that as the reader will see later on in this chapter.

Original Song Title was Different

As in the immortal words of the film *The Quiet Man* we must begin at the beginning. The beginning was when Larry Cunningham's mother, Julia Cosgrove, and Philip (Phil) Fitzpatrick were friends in Leitrim's Aughavas area and she started to sing his song.

Larry Cunningham thinks that his mother and Phil Fitzpatrick may have been going out together long before she moved to Longford and met and married his father. 'She told me that it was from him that she got the words, because obviously at that time it had never been recorded. As far as I know it was my mother and he who put an air to it then. I know that the original air might resemble something else but perhaps that helped its popularity too. Often when a song resembles some other tune it's easier to remember. It was a *sean nós* song at the time I got it from her. But of course I changed it to make it suitable for playing by a showband,' he adds.

In a typewritten sheet which the Fitzpatrick family have in their bar in Mohill, the song is credited as being the same air as 'The Flower of Sweet Strabane'. The six verses of the song are typed on this sheet using an old manual typewriter and it is possible this was done during Phil Fitzpatrick's lifetime. According to that sheet the original title of the song was 'Where Shannon Waters Flow'. Larry learned the song from his mother after he heard her sing it at his brother's wedding. 'It was in the very early 1960s, Lord rest my brother Michael, it was at his wedding that she sang it *sean nós* style. That was the first time I heard it and the song struck a chord with me. But of course it was not accepted at the time that a showband would have an old Irish ballad in a dance programme.'

Wrong Side Would Be Right Side!

Larry seems to have left 'Lovely Leitrim' dormant for a few years as he did not start singing it on stage until after he had his first hit with 'Tribute to Jim Reeves'. It was also far away from Leitrim that he first sang the song on stage.

'We tried it out first during a tour of England. I felt that this would be the best place to perform it, as we were entertaining emigrants who might have an affinity with the words. I got a good clap for the song and that was encouraging.' But even when playing for the Irish in Britain Larry still did not perform the song as part of the band's mainstream dance programme. 'At that time there were no relief bands and four of us would keep the show going while the other four went for a cup of coffee or a smoke during the break. Nobody took much notice of what you did during these breaks,' he adds.

Prior to this Larry had changed the tempo of the song from its original *sean nós* style. He says that *sean nós* has no tempo and it is up to the singer to put the quivers into it when performing. To make it into a number for a dancing programme it had to be changed to an old-time waltz, which is also known as 3/4 time.

'Every time I sang it there were more people asking for the song the next time we played the same venue. I can't say that I knew it would be a hit but I guessed that it had something special and I felt comfortable singing it. However it still could not be included when the full band were on stage.'

So in its seminal stage 'Lovely Leitrim' was still no more than another number to be played during break-time for some of the band. Larry decided that as it had gone down so well during the breaks at dances in England it was worth trying it out in similar situations at home. After getting a good reaction at the dances around Ireland the Mighty Avons decided that it was worth putting it on the 'B' side of a record. But this tells its own tale, as the 'B' side of singles usually got very few plays on radio! However 'Lovely Leitrim' proved that 'the wrong side would be the right side.' Similarly another 'B' side, 'Gentle Mother' by Big Tom and the Mainliners, would buck the trend shortly afterwards.

Sex, Country 'n' Irish and Gay Byrne

The recording session took place in Eamonn Andrews' Studio in Dublin and the man in charge was the popular arranger-producer Noel Kelehan, also well known for his work with RTÉ. Even though it was only going to be on the flipside of 'There's that Smile Again', it still appears that great care was taken with the recording.

Noel Kelehan had his own ideas about adding luscious strings to the backing to give it an orchestral feel. 'He hired members of the RTÉ Light Orchestra to play on it. There were four of them. But Noel probably used some multi-tracking technique to make it sound as if there were eight violins playing on it. If my recollection is right some of those playing in the backing were not even Irish. But that did not prevent them from having a great feel for what we were recording. They did not have to be from Drumshanbo to give it their all,' laughs Larry. It did not take very long to record the song either according to him. Larry still had memories of the 50 times he sang 'Tribute to Jim Reeves' at his first recording session. But he says this one was recorded 'in one or two takes'.

There is a saying in Ireland that there was no sex in the country until Gay Byrne hit the black and white TV screens with *The Late Late Show* in the 1960s! But perhaps Gaybo, as he is affectionately known, may have also unwittingly helped unleash the musical genre known as 'Country 'n' Irish'?

'Leitrim is one of the home counties of Country and Irish music, a genre which has its stronghold in the border areas and the midlands.' So states Damien Corless in one of his less derogatory remarks about this form of music on the Ian Gallagher website (www.iangallagher.com/country). If Leitrim is one of the home counties of this form of music then undoubtedly one could credit 'Lovely Leitrim' as being the first Country 'n' Irish hit.

Gay Byrne may well be one presenter who can take some of the credit or blame for this. Larry Cunningham has never forgotten how one play helped his song to chart success. 'At that time Gay Byrne presented the charts programme on Radio Éireann and he also presented the popular *Hospitals Requests* show. Our single 'There's that Smile Again' made it into the charts but when it went to about Number 5 I figured that was as far as it was going to go. It was on a Wednesday that the 'B' side got a play from Gay Byrne on the *Hospitals Requests* show. Back then if you got a play on that programme it was recognised as one of the best plays you could get on radio.

'By the time the charts show came up the following Monday all the records we had in the shops were sold. While "There's that Smile Again" had been on the way out, Gay Byrne said that if there were enough records available the

'Lovely Leitrim' side would be in the charts. By the following week it was in there on the hit parade. The record company manufactured a new supply of discs. They were snapped up in the shops and it went to Number One. The rest is history,' says Larry in a nonchalant way. The record went on to sell over a quarter of a million copies. 'It sold £10,000 worth of records in bad times,' stated Larry in an interview with Eddie Coffey in 1987 (*The Longford Leader,* 19 June 1987).

'Lovely Leitrim' became a career song for Larry and the Mighty Avons. It sustained the momentum for them in the charts after their first two hits with 'Tribute to Jim Reeves' and 'I Guess I'm Crazy'. 'The 'Lovely Leitrim' formula was to be repeated hundreds of times over the next two decades as songwriters, hoping to cash in on Cunningham's success, quickly wrote of the charms and attractions of every crossroads, townland and county in the nation,' wrote Paschal Mooney. (*The Swingin' Sixties* – Coughlan Publishing 1990, p.90)

Paving the way for U2, The Sawdoctors or The Pogues!

Everywhere the crowds flocked to see Larry and the Mighty Avons and the fee that the band could command increased fourfold. But how did they manage to replicate on stage the orchestral sounds that were in the backing music on the record?

'We didn't and we simply couldn't do it at that time. Later

on of course you could have the sound of strings on keyboards but not back then. So we had to make do with what we had and I think we managed well enough with the rhythm section, piano and the brass players in our band. We had no problems at all with the dancing fans accepting it either at home or in the UK or America,' he says.

It also helped secure the release of an album in America on the Coral label titled 'The Two Sides of Larry Cunningham'. The sleeve notes on this album reveal that this song may have kick-started his career among the Irish in America. 'His single recording of "Lovely Leitrim" hit the No.1 spot on the Irish best-selling charts before its release in this country. It moved US record buyers to ask for more from this talented young son of Erin,' states the notes.

Both at home and abroad, particularly in the USA, Larry had to sing the song many times every night they took to the stage. Larry laughs heartily as he recalls the reaction of one member of his band to the number of times he would have to sing the song. 'As it got more popular there were times when I had to sing it up to six times a night. The late Paddy Smith from our brass section would measure the popularity of the band at different venues by the number of times I had to sing 'Lovely Leitrim'.

I remember playing in The City Centre Ballroom, New York and Paddy going into the dressing room to have a cigarette while I was singing the song. Paddy liked his cigarette and he was pleased to stay offstage and smoke three that night while I had to sing it six times. On other occasions when we would be coming home from gigs where the song proved less popular, Paddy would say that we were losing it as "Cunningham had only to sing the song twice that night"!

It may, as one newspaper article suggests, have also got some of the Irish emigrants buying records by other singers from the 'ould sod'. This practice may have transcended the generations with their children and grandchildren developing an interest in the music of U2, The Sawdoctors or The Pogues.

Writing in *The Longford News* Eugene McGloin tried to analyse the influence of Larry Cunningham on the record-buying habits of Irish emigrants. 'How could anybody be influenced by Larry Cunningham? The answer is simple. The poet Gerard Dawe spoke in one of his works about how the emigrating Irish survived in the "new world" by feeding themselves on images of what they left behind.' (*The Longford News*, 6 September 1985).

'Lovely Leitrim' certainly conjured up such images of home for the 1960s generation of Irish emigrants.

The 'Bing Crosby' of Leitrim

However Larry feels that the success of the song was not just because it was about Leitrim. The sentiments expressed in the lyrics were relevant to people from any county.

'Perhaps the fact that it was an Irish ballad which sounded

pleasant and easy on the ears may have helped. The punters just liked the sound of it. Of course I must give credit to Leitrim people for the way they supported it both at home and abroad. Longford and Cavan people quickly rowed in behind it too,' he recalls.

Larry adds that while Leitrim has the shortest Atlantic coastline of any county, this short shoreline is still used to promote the fact that the county is lovely! 'The coastline of Leitrim must be only about a hundred yards long. It touches the sea close to Bundoran, and fair play to the county council, the road sign there states 'Welcome to Lovely Leitrim'. This is good marketing for both the county and the song'. In his collection of newspaper cuttings Larry displays one faded-to-brown disintegrating piece of newsprint. It is cut from a page of *The Leitrim Observer* on a date unknown during 1966. The impression made by the type on the paper via old-style hot metal type, set in an era prior to modern newspaper printing, is erratic. But in spite of the poor printing quality the message is clear. Larry Cunningham was the toast of a meeting of Leitrim County Council in 1966.

The Chairman of the County Council, P.L. Coyle, praised Larry for keeping Leitrim in the news, which he said was good from a tourist point of view. In seconding the Chairman's motion another member of the council, R. Ellis, said it was the first time he knew the Chairman was a 'Pop' man. 'This fine song has been in existence for a long time, but this is the first time it got into the Top Ten'. The Chairman responded by saying that Bing Crosby by his rendering of 'Galway Bay' made

Galway into the popular resort that it is. 'Perhaps Larry Cunningham can do the same for Leitrim,' he added (*The Leitrim Observer* 1966).

In 2009 Leitrim historian John Bredin from Carrick-on-Shannon says Larry Cunningham is still a star attraction at the Leitrim Roots Festival, which attracts tourists annually from all over the world.

Larry's Mother Says Song Will Lose its Worth

Larry Cunningham sang 'Lovely Leitrim' on so many TV shows around the time it was a hit that he can't remember which show he sang it on first. 'There were so many of them that time and in the following years that I lost count of all the times I did it on TV,' he claims. But he has particularly good memories of singing it on a *Trom agus Eadtrom* TV show recorded in Drumshanbo. 'I think that was recorded in the Mayflower Ballroom and that Thelma Mansfield was the presenter. There was a great atmosphere there on that night and everybody sang along. But no matter where we sang it people joined in. It was such a simple song to remember, the words were easily memorised. On nights when we had to sing it four or five times everybody knew the words by the end of the show. To this very day audiences are still singing it with me,' exclaims Larry with a laugh.

Just as some of the Mighty Avons were not initially

enthusiastic about 'Tribute to Jim Reeves', Larry says they were not overly enthusiastic either about 'Lovely Leitrim'. 'But the song fought its own battle and its popularity instilled in everybody that it was the song to sing. Whether all my band liked it or not didn't matter as I knew once it took off that everybody wanted it.'

But Larry had to do a bit of hard selling to convince his mother about the way he was changing the song that she had sung for so long. 'My mother thought that because I was changing the tempo the song would lose its worth and appeal. I had to explain to her that there was no way I could have done it the way she was singing it. My sound and hers were two completely different sounds. Her version was *sean nós* style, sung in a slow way without any musical accompaniment. It was beautiful and it was her singing style that attracted me to it initially,' he says with respect for the original version. But he adds that he knew he would have to 'fiddle around with it' to make it suitable for playing on a showband programme.

Both his parents were alive when 'Lovely Leitrim' was at No 1 and there is no doubt that Larry was very proud of this. He seems especially happy that his mother not alone saw its success, but shared a little of the limelight later on. 'When she would go on holidays to Bundoran, which was her favourite place, she was more popular than I was. She would sometimes stay with members of the great céilí band there, the Fitzgeralds. When she would get up and sing with some of them she was the real "Lovely Leitrim" star,' he laughs.

Sad Prophetic Verses

Perhaps as she sang the song, the same way as in her youth, Larry's mother's mind wandered back to the time when she and Phil Fitzpatrick performed it at house dances. Decades later a poem published in *The Leitrim Observer* also praised Phil Fitzpatrick as one of Leitrim's young freedom fighters during the War of Independence.

> *He bravely played a soldier's part,*
> *No plate his breast did shield;*
> *And sadly did his comrades fall,*
> *By Selton's battlefield.*
> *But though the grass be coloured red,*
> *Where Irish blood did flow;*
> *The foes did feel his lead and steel,*
> *Through hills and valleys low.*
>
> – Matt Tiernan, Cornulla, Cloone

It seems that after the Irish War of Independence the 'Lovely Leitrim' man took the emigrant ship to the USA like so many of his generation. His sister Nan was already in New York and recording songs for the Columbia label there. Among the 78 records she made was the emigration song 'Far Away in Australia' which has a lot of resonance with many who left Leitrim for the land 'down under'.

'All the Irish stores in America sold my records,' stated Nan in a newspaper interview decades after she had returned to Leitrim. She was then a 74-year-old grandmother, Nan Gaffney, from Ballinamore. But her brother Phil was not lucky enough to make it back to his 'Lovely Leitrim'. One verse of the poem in his honour by Matt Tiernan tells of his move across the Atlantic in the early 1920s.

He sailed away to America,
The land beyond the foam;
Where thousands of our country's youth,
Were forced to take a home.

That same poem also charts his success in getting employment in the Big Apple as a member of the forces of law and order.

A mounted cop who made the top,
For many a weary day;
Around Central Park by light, by dark;
In that land so far away.

Even though absorbed by his work as a policeman, and devoted to his wife Mary and their five sons, Phil Fitzpatrick still found time to pen poems and songs. 'He was blessed with the gift of poetry. He also had the stout heart of a police officer who when duty called feared not the moment,' states a story in the New York's Police magazine *Spring 3100*.

Beside this story is one of the poems that he wrote long

after he penned 'Lovely Leitrim'. It is entitled 'The New York Police' and some of the lines were sadly prophetic for him.

> *A policeman is always on duty,*
> *He has goodness and kindness in store;*
> *When he kisses his wife and children goodbye,*
> *There's a chance he will see them no more.'*

(*Spring 3100* June 1947
New York Police Publications, p. 47)

Similar to his most famous song 'Lovely Leitrim', this one also has six verses and all were published in the June 1947 New York police magazine.

Now for the first time this book publishes all original six verses of 'Lovely Leitrim' or 'Where Shannon Waters Flow'. The two verses not recorded by Larry Cunningham are numbered four and five. 'There was no chance that a six-verse song would be played as a record on Radio Éireann at the time it was released. But it might have been different if we were releasing it during the days of the pirate radio stations in Ireland.

A funny story is often told about how one pirate DJ played all one side of an artist's album without any interruption for talk between the tracks. The singer rang him up and made a jocose remark that he might play the other side of the album on his show the next day,' laughs Larry.

No Time for Laughs . . . Time for Tears

But it was no laughing matter for him and the Mighty Avons when it came to the time for deciding which verses of 'Lovely Leitrim' they should leave out.

'Unless I sang the last verse the song would lose its meaning. So we had to opt to leave verses four and five out. To this day I still think they were the two best verses and I'm glad that they are finally being published in this book,' says Larry. The song title was also changed to 'Lovely Leitrim'.

Those familiar with Larry Cunningham's version of the song will note that he also made several other minor word changes to it.

'Apart from having to drop the two verses I suppose another big change I made was in the first verse. I changed the words 'native Leitrim' to 'lovely Leitrim'. I was not a native of Leitrim so why should I say so in a song,' is Larry's reason for this change.

One wonders what would Phil Fitzpatrick have thought about the changes and the omission of the two verses.

Where Shannon Waters Flow (Air: *The Flower of Sweet Strabane*)

By Philip Fitzpatrick

I

Last night I had a pleasant dream
I woke up with a smile
I dreamt that I was back again
In dear old Erin's isle
I thought I saw Lough Allen's banks
In the valley down below
It was my native Leitrim
Where Shannon waters flow.

II

Now I felt enchanted with this scene
Of grandeur and delight
So I travelled off to Carrick town
Before the dark of night
I passed Sheemore, that fairy hill
Where flowers fine do grow
And I saw the grave of Finn McCool
Where Shannon Waters flow.

III

I next did visit Fenagh town
And her ancient abbey walls
Where the teachings of the holy monks
Once echoed through her halls.
I stood with reverence on this spot
Reluctant for to go
From this town of saints and sages
Where Shannon waters flow.

IV

My eyes are dim and wet with tears
I must be dreaming still
For I thought I saw those heroes
Who died on Selton Hill.
Now the fog is lifting from the scene
And I am forced to go
And leave this land so beautiful
Where Shannon waters flow.

V

The Englishman drinks to the rose
The Scotsman the bluebell
With pride they toast their countries
And great deeds of valour tell.
But give me Ireland's shamrock green
That abundantly does grow
On the fertile plains of Leitrim
Where Shannon waters flow.

VI

I've travelled far in many lands
Throughout the east and west
Of all the lands I've travelled o'er
I love my own the best.
And if ever I return again
The first place that I'll go
Will be to lovely Leitrim
Where Shannon waters flow.

(The two verses IV & V omitted in the hit record are printed above in **bold**)

Bloody Deaths and 'The Streets of New York'

Phil Fitzpatrick was a brave officer. Perhaps the training as a volunteer soldier around the hills and valleys of his lovely Leitrim during the fight for Irish freedom was a good apprenticeship. He did not fear facing down the thugs and criminals, while either on or off duty around the streets of New York. On a fateful day in May 1947 his chances of ever seeing his native lovely Leitrim again were cruelly taken away. 'Patrolman Fitzpatrick and another off-duty patrolman were having lunch at a bar and grill on East 96th Street and 3rd Avenue when two men entered and announced a hold-up.' (The Officer Down Memorial Page, Inc website). According to this page on the internet the bloody events unfolded on Tuesday 20 May 1947.

Obviously it was just another afternoon of serving lunches, chat and the mundane clatter of cups, plates and cutlery for those at the bar and grill. Then suddenly everything was to change and chaos reigned supreme. Two men, one wielding a .32 calibre revolver, burst into the bar and grill and ordered the patrons to the rear of the premises. The moments of high drama are related in detail in the New York Police Officers' magazine *Spring 3100* of June of that year.

'Patrolman Fitzpatrick, in defiance of the edict, lunged at the holder of the gun, later identified as Ernest De Ratier (23), and attempted to disarm him of the weapon. The bandit, at point-blank range fired twice, both slugs finding their mark in Fitzpatrick's abdomen. Patrolman Dammeyer in the meantime had drawn his own weapon and discharged three shots at De Ratier, killing him instantly. He fired two more at the second thug, afterwards identified as Joseph Maglio (30). He had jumped from behind the bar where he was emptying the cash register and making for the door.' (*Spring 3100* June 1947 New York Police Publications, p. 2).

The magazine's account of the incident also states that the second thug (Maglio) died two hours later at Beth David Hospital, Manhattan. As his life's blood streamed from his wounds Phil Fitzpatrick was also rushed to the same hospital. After two days of blood transfusions he was taken off the critical list and hopes were high for his recovery. But sadly this was not to happen.

'Suffering a sudden relapse after lingering for six days with two slugs from the ex-convict's gun in his abdomen, Patrolman Philip Fitzpatrick died at 2.55 p.m. on Monday May 26. He had fought bravely that he might live.' (*Spring 3100* June 1947 New York Police Publications, p.2).

Subsequent investigations revealed that the two thugs had long criminal records. De Ratier, who fired the fatal shots at Phil Fitzpatrick, was out on bail at the time after committing another robbery at gunpoint two months earlier. Less than an hour before he mortally wounded the 'Lovely Leitrim' songwriter, De Ratier was also one of a group of thugs who robbed another bar and grill in Manhattan. They had escaped with $190.

Phil Fitzpatrick left a wife (Mary) and five sons. At the time of his passing his son Charles (23) was also a patrolman in the

New York Police. His other sons were James (24), Philip (17), John (15) and Peter (13). His parents Rose and James were still alive as were his five brothers and three sisters.

> *When the sad news reached his parents dear,*
> *Their hair now turning grey;*
> *It brought them back sad memories,*
> *Of the day he went away.'*
>
> – Matt Tiernan, Cornulla, Cloone

The slaying of Patrolman Phil Fitzpatrick (49) in 1947 has strange similarities with the fate that was to befall the fictitious Irish-born policeman 'Benjy' in the song 'The Streets of New York'. But it was written decades later by Liam Reilly of Bagatelle and reached No 1 for the Wolfe Tones in 1981.

> *'At the time uncle Benjy was a policeman in Brooklyn...*
> *Well to shorten the story I found out that day.*
> *That Benjy was shot down in an uptown foray.'*
> (Liam Reilly).

The *Spring 3100* magazine of June 1947 states that massive crowds turned out to pay their last respects to this brave son of Leitrim. The funeral of Patrolman Fitzpatrick was attended by Mayor William O'Dwyer of New York and many other dignitaries.

Mayor William O'Dwyer, the 100th Mayor of New York 1946-50, was born and raised in Bohola, County Mayo, Ireland. He served as a policeman before studying law. He was a brother of Paul O'Dwyer, liberal activist, lawyer, Democratic politician and founder of the O'Dwyer Cheshire Home, Bohola. Prior to being elected mayor, William O'Dwyer was King's County District Attorney in the US in 1939. His prosecution of the organised crime syndicate, Murder Inc., made him a national celebrity as a tough crime fighter. However after being appointed as Ambassador to Mexico by President Harry Truman in 1950 he had to return to New York to answer questions about his own association with organised crime figures. These accusations followed him to the grave in 1964 when he was buried in Arlington National Cemetery – close to the grave of a very famous Irish-American laid to rest there just a few months earlier – President John F. Kennedy. Mayor William O'Dwyer, who like Phil Fitzpatrick, was Irish, was no stranger to dealing with crime and criminals, including murderers.

'Patrolman Fitzpatrick was posthumously awarded the New York City Police Department's Medal of Honour for his actions. He had served with the New York City Police Department for 21 years. (The Officer Down Memorial Page, Inc. website)

Faithful Horse with Head Bowed

Phil Fitzpatrick was laid to rest in St John's Cemetery, Middle Village, Queens. It's a resting place far from the friendly fields of his lovely Leitrim, which he immortalised in his song.

How prophetic the following few lines, culled from another poem *A Part of America Died* were to be for the writer Phil Fitzpatrick.

Somebody killed a policeman today
And a part of America died.
A piece of our country he swore to protect,
Will be buried with him at his side.

The final few lines of Phil's poem could easily have been written as a premonition of his own fate.

A cop put his life on the line.
Now his ghost walks a beat on a dark city street,
And he stands at each rookie's side.
He answered the call, and gave it his all,
And a part of America died.

By Philip Fitzpatrick. Badge No. 153488
City of N.Y. Police Department. Mounted Division.

It is understood that the faithful steed of Phil Fitzpatrick was part of his huge funeral parade. Larry Cunningham says he has been told that even the horse seemed to be in mourning for its master.

'It is said, even though I've not seen it written, that the horse was given some sort of a sedative. This is supposed to have resulted in him following in the cortege with his head bowed.'

Today a monument, erected in 1936, stands to the memory of Phil's comrades who were slain on Selton Hill. In Mohill, where members of his extended family operate a very successful bar and lounge, there is a memorial nearby to commemorate another great musician. That memorial, unveiled by President Patrick Hillary in 1986, is to commemorate Turlough O'Carolan (1670-1738). He was a great composer of music for the harp. He lived at Mohill around 1720, and it was here his family members were reared. This blind entertainer made his living by playing the harp and composing musical pieces. The men who fell at Selton Hill devoted their lives to the fight for liberty and O'Carolan devoted his life to making music. Philip Fitzpatrick devoted his life to both music and the fight for liberty, here in Ireland and in 'the land of liberty'.

Perhaps some day a memorial in his honour will be on the streetscape in Mohill, Ballinamore or elsewhere. Or in a rural location its shadow may fall across the willows or rushes that are home to the harmless slimy slugs in the green fields of his 'Lovely Leitrim'. In the meantime, and possibly forever, Larry Cunningham's abridged version of his song will perpetuate the songwriting talents of this brave 'Lovely Leitrim' man.

Six

Carnegie Hall via the local Post Office!

Bill Fuller was a leading American-based music promoter. Once he was asked if he wished to meet Elvis, the King of Rock 'n' Roll. He is reputed to have answered, 'f . . k Elvis'. Imagine the same promoter telephoning a rural post office in County Longford to book Irish Country King Larry Cunningham to play a concert in New York's famous Carnegie Hall.

This extraordinary event happened in the mid 1960s. Promoter Fuller rang Granard Post Office. By a happy coincidence it was Larry Cunningham and not Elvis that was leaving the building!

This happened around the same time that Fuller was less complimentary to Elvis as explained later in this chapter.

It was such a coincidence, almost like being struck by lightning, that Larry was in the post office at that moment. He had been buying some stamps and posting letters when Fuller made the transatlantic telephone call.

Larry was a big singing star in Ireland at that time and the girls behind the post office counter were delighted to see him. They chatted about where he had been playing the night before. Indeed the additional time spent talking with him may have resulted in him being delayed long enough to be in the right place at the right time to take Bill Fuller's call.

It was a time in rural Ireland when virtually no private house, except the local doctor, priest or shopkeeper had a phone. Much of the communication was via the post offices, all of which had phones and operated a telegram service. Like most rural dwellers Larry Cunningham relied heavily on his local post office for communications with the outside world.

But on that day this line of communication was to be more significant than ever for the singing star. As he was leaving the building one of the ladies working behind the counter followed him to his car. Excitedly she said there was a phone call from America for him at that very moment.

Larry says he did not believe her at first and he reluctantly went back into the building with her and gingerly took up the receiver.

Larry still laughs when he recalls how he was sure it was somebody putting on an accent similar to that of Bill Fuller. 'Tis me that's in it,' said the voice.

He was vaguely familiar with the Irish-American promoter's voice from listening to others imitating his way of speaking. He spoke in tones tinged with a native Kerry slant intermingled with more recently acquired American nuances.

'Even when the soft-spoken voice on the other end of the line asked me why I would not play Carnegie Hall for him I was still sceptical. I thought it was somebody playing a joke on me.'

One gets the impression that Larry may have been inclined to tell the caller to 'f . . . off'. But if so it seems that he held back on making any such utterance. As the phone call progressed the young singer realised that his management, and perhaps even some members of his band, had failed to inform him of a possible prestige date. It was regarding a show on the following St Patrick's Night in New York's Carnegie Hall.

Carnegie Hall – a World Famous Venue

Carnegie Hall is one of the world's most famous concert halls and its stages have been graced by many of history's greatest artists and public figures.

'Opened in 1891 it is known for its excellent acoustics and extravagant architecture On 5 May 1891 hundreds of New Yorkers jammed the concert hall to see the great composer Peter Ilyich Tchaikovsky play there,' states the website www.manhattan.about.com. It also states that the construction of Carnegie Hall, begun in 1890, was financed by Andrew Carnegie, one of the richest men of the time. You can still see the words 'Music Hall founded by Andrew Carnegie' on the facade of the building.

The building's chief architect was William Burnet Tuthill, who, according to the website, chose an Italian Renaissance style. Inside, the elegant foyer is a vision of marble and intricately carved columns.

The Carnegie family owned Carnegie Hall until 1925 and even after passing on to different owners it remained one of New York's premier concert halls. But by 1960 it was under threat of closure until the City of New York bought the site for five million dollars.

It was taken over by the non-profit Carnegie Hall Corporation who continue to run the venue. In 1964, a few years before Larry Cunningham played there for the first time, it was designated a National Historical Landmark.

The Irish singing star may not have known much of its illustrious history at the time that he got the transatlantic phone call to play Carnegie Hall. But Larry Cunningham knew that only a select few of his peers, even in the country music industry in America, had the honour of playing there.

Some singers got slated in the media for even attempting to bring country music to this hallowed stage. Other major names in American country music were overawed and performed poorly there as explained later in this chapter.

But this fledgling country singer from Longford was not overawed by the challenge. It seems Larry relished the idea of gracing the stage of this famous concert hall.

Larry – In The Dark

'In reply to what Bill was saying to me on the phone I admitted that playing Carnegie Hall was something that I could only dream about,' says Larry. 'But to this he replied that he had phoned my management a month earlier to see if I could play a concert there on the following St Patrick's Night. But it seems he was told that I could not do it, as I was booked for a dance in Castlerea, County Roscommon that night. He was left waiting for a reply to his offer of a date instead in Carnegie Hall.

'Well you can imagine the ambition that I had to play in Carnegie Hall and how excited I got when I knew that phone call was genuine. Many of my heroes such as Jim Reeves and Buck Owens had played there.' According to Larry he told Bill Fuller to 'write down' his name immediately and he would be there.

'I said don't worry about the dance in Castlerea. I will be in New York on that night and I don't care what band is with me,' says Larry.

As far as he can recall, this phone call was made in November or December. It was during the height of the showband era. Back then dates for bands such as Larry and the Mighty Avons would be booked for shows up to a year ahead of such events.

One gets the impression that Larry was willing to let the Mighty Avons off to play in Castlerea without him on the following St Patrick's Night. He would work with any backing group just for the honour of playing Carnegie Hall.

It emerged that Bill Fuller's wife at that time, the popular Irish-American singer Carmel Quinn, was originally booked for the date. But as she was pregnant she was not going to be able to perform at Carnegie Hall that night and Larry was suggested as her replacement.

She came to fame on TV in the US in the late 1950s and 1960s. She had entertained Presidents John F. Kennedy and Lyndon B. Johnson at The White House. She also consistently sold out annual St Patrick's Night concerts at Carnegie Hall for many years.

But as Larry was being touted as her replacement it seems some of those around him were not very enthusiastic about the idea. Even today one gets the impression that Larry is still annoyed about this. It seems some of those around him in his band and management had kept the possibility of the Carnegie Hall date a secret from him. But perhaps it is blind loyalty to those who worked with him then, some who have since passed on, that he is still reluctant, even now over forty years later, to criticise them. One can only surmise his feelings about being almost deprived of one of the most prestigious concert dates in his music career.

No doubt some strong words were said when Larry told the others members of the Mighty Avons of his views on the New York gig. His management and band were told he would be playing Carnegie Hall on the following St Patrick's Night, 1967, irrespective of where they would be!

'I was working with the lads a few nights after the phone call from Bill Fuller when I told them about it. It was following a dance and there was complete and utter silence in the dressing room when I told them what I was going to do.

'I just said to them that I did not care what they were going to do, but I was going to be in Carnegie Hall. Mr Fuller had told me that he would have a band there and it would be no problem even if my band did not travel.'

One could suggest that either Larry's management and/or perhaps some of the band members had viewed the offer differently. The possibility of the large crowd of dancers they could attract to the ballroom in Castlerea was attractive financially. So what for the prestige of playing at one of America's most famous venues, Carnegie Hall? But obviously this was not Larry's way of thinking.

'I could go on and on about what was said, but I don't want to. All I will say is that eventually the entire band agreed to come with me and Bill Fuller allowed them to come,' recalls Larry.

Bill Fuller – An Enigma

All this suggests that Bill Fuller was not impressed with the way some of the people around Larry had failed to tell him about the Carnegie Hall date. Fuller was a larger-than-life character. Born in Kerry he emigrated to London as a teenager and first became wealthy in the construction industry. He later got involved in the ballroom and hotel business in the UK, Ireland and the USA.

Among his venues were The Old Sheiling Hotel in Raheny, Dublin and Teach Furbo (now the Connemara Coast Hotel) in Connemara where all the top ballad groups of the mid-1960s played.

In England he owned venues including The Apollo in Manchester, and a once very rough venue known as The Buffalo in London's Camden Town. His ballrooms in Ireland included the Town and Country and The Crystal in Dublin and The Atlantic in Tramore, County Waterford. When he moved to the USA he became successful in a variety of businesses. His business empire ranged from owning ballrooms and rock venues in New York to gold mines in Las Vegas.

During his long career Fuller was well known and respected as an entertainment promoter. He died in the summer of 2008 at the age of 91. He gained notoriety even in his latter years for having bankrolled bail for a stripper in a high-profile murder case in Las Vegas. The girl was Sandy Murphy and he came up with over two million dollars in legal fees to help have her acquitted of a murder charge.

'After a lifetime of avoiding publicity, he was suddenly thrust into the media spotlight at the age of 82. That was when he posted bail and paid extensive legal fees for Sandy Murphy,' states an article in *The Guardian* newspaper in September 2008.

It also states that Sandy Murphy was a Las Vegas stripper who was charged with murdering a wealthy casino owner. 'Fuller said he was simply drawn to Murphy by her surname and an absolute conviction that she was innocent.' (Guardian.co.uk)

According to a story by Liam Collins in the *Sunday Independent*, 3 August 2008, at the height of his career Fuller owned 26 ballrooms. He also had a construction company that employed 3,000 people. In another story in *The Guardian* newspaper he is cited as having amassed some of his fortune from demolition work in the UK. Indeed there was a saying about him at the time: 'What Hitler didn't knock down, Bill Fuller did.' (*The Guardian*, 9 September 2008)

'He moved to Las Vegas at a time when Brendan Bowyer and the Big 8 had started a tradition of Irish acts spending part of the year in the famous gambling city controlled by the Mafia,' states the story by Liam Collins in the *Sunday Independent*.

According to the same writer Fuller intervened in a dangerous situation at one of the venues that he owned, The Old Sheiling Hotel, Raheny, Dublin, many years earlier. It was after a drunken woman climbed up on the stage. She got a shove from one of the musicians that sent her sprawling back into the body of the hall.

'It was like a spark and the whole place erupted into fighting, like a scene from *The Quiet Man*. Then suddenly in the middle of the mêlée came Bill Fuller. With a couple of well-aimed punches, he flattened three or four of the main protagonists, men and women alike. As suddenly as the trouble began, peace descended and the event resumed. Mr Fuller walked nonchalantly back to his office – a hard man in a tough business,' concludes the Liam Collins' story.

The same story notes that a Dublin promoter claimed Fuller was 'a mate of the Mafia' in Las Vegas. It added that the musicians' union was so strong there it was difficult to get work for outside musicians in the city. But he had the musicians' union 'squared' according to the article. However musician Paddy Cole (ex Big 8 showband) is quoted as being 'more circumspect'. He says Fuller was 'well connected' and had 'ways and means' of getting around the musicians' union ban on outside musicians. (Liam Collins *Sunday Independent,* 3 August 2008).

Much earlier in Fuller's career, when he was only 20, he took over a notorious rough house, The Buffalo Ballroom in Camden Town. In more recent times this venue came to fame in rock music circles as The Electric Ballroom.

According to another part of the article on Bill Fuller in *The Guardian* newspaper of 9 September 2008, The Buffalo had been forcibly closed down before Fuller bought it.

'A keen amateur boxer and wrestler Fuller persuaded the local police chief to let him reopen it. He promised that if he ever needed to call the constabulary he would close the hall down for good. Fuller manned the door himself and transformed The Buffalo into one of the most popular Irish ballrooms in the country.' (*The Guardian,* 9 September 2008). The same story maintains that apart from all his venues, Fuller also operated a management and promotions company whose list of clients in the 1960s included Johnny Cash, Patsy Cline, Billie Holiday and Joe Loss.

So one gets the impression that if this promoter wanted somebody such as Larry Cunningham to play in Carnegie Hall, he was going to get his way. The views of Larry's management or band members may not have mattered to Fuller.

The Carnegie Hall Concert

According to Larry he was delighted when his entire band agreed to play the Carnegie Hall show with him. But if they did not, Fuller would have provided a backing band anyway.

'It was just great that my entire band came with me because I knew then that I would have no reason to be nervous. The people around me were the group of lads who knew exactly what programme of songs I was going to do. I was very happy about this. I remember that on the night there was a lovely band from Wexford as one of the support acts and our guest artist was the late Tommy Makem, one of Ireland's greatest Folk stars.'

Larry claims they had played to bigger crowds in some other venues but to play Carnegie Hall was one of the highlights of his career. He was impressed by the layout of the building, especially the balcony and the huge stage. He

FAMILY TRADITION: Larry enjoying a session of music and song at home with his mother Julia (Cosgrove) Cunningham and his grandfather Michael Cosgrove.

FIRST BAND: Larry with two members of the Grafton Showband, the late Seamus Reilly and the late Josie Feeney.

LARRY and the MIGHTY AVONS

FULL TIME: Larry (third from left) with the Mighty Avons. From left, Paddy Smith (RIP), Peter Smith, Brian Finlay (RIP), Ronnie Griffiths, Gerry Walshe (RIP) and Jimmy Smith.

A DISASTER! The first date for Larry and the Mighty Avons in the Granada Ballroom, Granard was a disaster for them. They weren't invited back to the Granada for quite some time!

LOCAL FOOTBALL:
Granard Minors, 1951.
Larry is second from right
(standing).

UK FOOTBALL
CHAMPIONS: Derby Senior
GAA team, 1956. Larry is
second from left at back.

THE HOUSE THAT LARRY BUILT: Back
from England Larry is pictured in front of
the house he built in 1960.

FUN TIME: Three members of the Mighty
Avons enjoy an informal music session as
they play their tin whistles. Micky Brady,
Jimmy Smith and Larry Cunningham.

JIM REEVES ADVERTISEMENT: An advertisement for the Jim Reeves show, supported by the Mighty Avons at the Orchard Ballroom, Lifford, County Donegal, 1963.

ORCHID Ballroom Lifford

Jim Reeves: Special Announcement

The proprietors of the Orchid Ballroom, Lifford, understand that many people who attended the JIM REEVES DANCE in The Orchid Ballroom last Friday were disappointed at the short duration of Mr. Reeves' appearance. We were disappointed also.

Mr. Reeves was contracted by us to appear for 30 to 45 minutes, as he is at each venue on his Irish tour. The brevity of his appearance was due to a fault and eventually the failure of the amplification system—circumstances entirely outside our control.

To compensate for any disappointment, the Proprietors of the Ballroom, in conjunction with Mr. Reeves and his London Agent, have decided to run a

FREE DANCE in the ORCHID BALLROOM, Lifford
ON FRIDAY NEXT, 14th JUNE, 1963.

when patrons will be assured of a most enjoyable evening.
Music by one of
Ireland's Leading Showbands — THE PACIFIC.

SUNDAY, 16th JUNE

Freshmen Showband

Dancing 9—1 a.m.

Admission — 5/-.

★

JIM REEVES APOLOGY: The following week the ballroom proprietors posted an apology for 'the brevity' of the Jim Reeves show.

REEVES THREATENS TO SUE: Jim Reeves' widow Mary and her second husband, Terry Davis. Mary autographed this photograph for Beatrice Cunningham at a time when she was threatening to sue the Irish singer.

LARRY AND LARRY: 'To make the British pop charts was phenomenal,' said top Irish radio presenter Larry Gogan pictured here with Larry Cunningham in the mid 1960s.

The Disc that wiped Everyone's Eye

Larry's Tribute to Jim

The disc that wiped everyone's eye. That's what they were saying about the Mighty Avons *Tribute to Jim Reeves*. There's been a lot of speculation during the past 12 months as to what Irish Showband would first crash the British record charts, and the Mighty Avons was certainly not one of the hottest tips.

In fact no one, not even the band themselves, had ever given much thought to the Cavan band cutting a record until Cyril Joyce, the small King John's Irish agent heard them one night.

He was particularly impressed with their *Tribute to Jim Reeves*, which he considered by far, the best of the many similar compositions he had heard. He later approached he band and they agreed to put the number on tape. Cyril then sent this over to the Company's London office with the note, "It's just a hunch—but I think this might be a winner."

Well it was. Released in England in the first week of November, it sold over 40,000 copies in the first two weeks alone. Many of the band's Irish fans weren't even aware they had cut a record until

they heard it on Luxemburg and Radio Caroline.

It was the least publicised Showband disc of the year, and it looked like being the most successful. The publicity came later of course, particularly here at home, where everyone suddenly began to sit up and take notice of a band that had been plodding along unspectacularly for so long.

UNCANNY

Larry Cunningham is the vocalist on both sides of the disc and his voice bears an uncanny resemblance to that of Reeves himself. Eddie

Masterson wrote the lyrics which incorporate part of the most Reeves songs, *He'll Have to Go, I Won't Forget You, Oh, How I Miss You To-Night, Adios Amigos*. Larry's treatment of *Take My Hand Precious Lord* on the flip is practically indistinguishable from Reeves' own version of the same number.

★

Larry who comes from Granard, Co. Longford has been singing with the Mighty Avons since the band was formed in Ballyhaise, Co. Cavan, in 1960. They have been fully professional since 1962.

POP STAR: *Spotlight* magazine, the publication known as the bible of Irish pop music in the 1960s, highlights Larry's unlikely hit in Britain.

UK POP CHARTS CLIMB: Making it into the UK Top 50 makes the headlines of the *Evening Herald*.

SILVER DISC: Larry proudly displays his award for sales of more than 250,000 copies of 'Tribute to Jim Reeves' in 1965.

UK AWARDS CELEBRATION: Larry and the Mighty Avons at the Silver Disc presentation in London in early 1965.

FIRST ALBUM: Larry's first album released on the King label in the UK and Ireland in 1966 and in the USA on the Coral label in 1967.

ALL TOGETHER: TV and radio sports presenter Jimmy Magee (front) with Larry, the Mighty Avons and road manager Mick Clerkin (extreme right) at the launch of one of their early singles.

CARNEGIE HALL: Playing at the prestigious New York venue was one of the highlights of Larry's career in the mid 1960s but it almost didn't happen until Larry had an important telephone conversation!

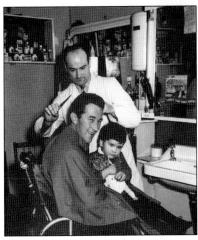

FRANK THE BARBER: Over the years Frank McMahon, Granard has been the only barber to style Larry Cunningham's hair and he continues to do so.
In this photo from the 1960s Larry is getting a trim with Frank's young daughter Ailish also in the photo.

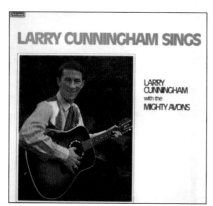

LARRY SOLD: As he planned to leave King Records, a number of Larry's recordings were sold to the EMI Label and the three albums pictured here were released in Ireland.

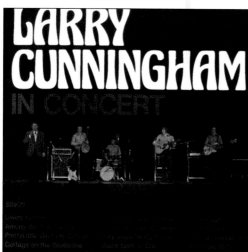

ONSTAGE IN THE USA: Larry pictured onstage at the Lincoln Centre, New York on the cover of his *In Concert* album.

LOVELY LEITRIM MAN: Phil Fitzpatrick who wrote 'Lovely Leitrim' pictured here in his New York police force uniform.

ON DUTY: Phil Fitzpatrick on horseback in New York's Central Park.

POLICE COLLEAGUES' TRIBUTE. Hundreds of police followed Phil Fitzpatrick's funeral cortège through the streets of New York, 1947. (Photos courtesy of Val Fitzpatrick and Mary Kennedy, Fitzpatrick's Céilí House, Mohill, County Leitrim.)

MAYOR AT SAD FAREWELL: Mayor William O'Dwyer of New York stands to attention, hat on heart, as Phil Fitzpatrick's coffin, draped in the American flag, is carried by his colleagues through the streets of New York, May 1947.

WEDDING DAY: Larry and Beatrice on their wedding day, 9 February 1972, with the chief celebrant at the ceremony, the bride's brother, Monsignor Bart Nannery.

INTERNATIONAL STAR: Larry is listed beside the big American Country stars at the Wembley International Festival of Country Music.

TOP OF THE BILL: A poster for Larry's sold-out concert at London's Royal Albert Hall in 1974.

LARRY AND MARGO: Year's before Larry and Margo worked together, UK magazine *Country Music People* previewed their individual appearances at the Wembley Country Festival.

REEVES REMEMBERED: Larry's tribute album to Jim Reeves was recorded in Nashville with musicians who worked with Jim and Elvis Presley.

A HIT AT WEMBLEY: Larry's album of songs fresh from Nashville was a big seller at the Wembley Country Festival in 1972.

ALL STARS: With one of the many Jimmy Magee All-Stars teams. Larry is first from left in the second row. Apart from being a fleet-footed footballer, the showbiz priest Fr Brian D'Arcy, (fourth from left at back) also looked after the spiritual needs of the showband members. He still celebrates a special mass once a year in County Longford for showband members living and deceased.

ONE OF THE BIGGEST: Among the many carnivals that Larry played at, the one at Stradone in Cavan was among the biggest. This advertisement from the *Anglo Celt* newspaper gives the reader a flavour of the many attractions at the event.

RAMBLIN' MAN POSTER: Larry's poster had a touch of the green, white and gold.

JETTING OFF: An appropriate album title and an appropriate photograph for this ramblin' Irishman.

NEW BAND: Larry's third band, the Country Blue Boys. Back row: Tony Treacy (RIP), Larry and Terry Reynolds. Front row: John McGarrigle, John Sheridan and Aidan Cunningham.

HOME TOWN HONOUR: Larry is presented with a certificate of congratulations by Granard Town Commissioners, 1977.

LARRY'S 21st: Larry and the original Mighty Avons onstage in Granard to celebrate his 21st anniversary in showbusiness.

INVITATION: The invitation card for Larry's 21st anniversary (front and inside) showing the list of special guests.

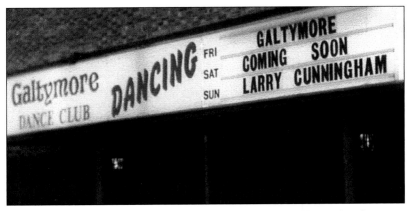

RECORD-BREAKING: The Galtymore Ballroom in London where Larry played to a record-breaking 6,850 fans.

TAOISEACH AND FRIENDS: Former Taoiseach Albert Reynolds launched one of Larry's albums on the K-Tel label. He is pictured here with Beatrice and Larry at the launch.

FREEDOM OF BOSTON: One of the citations proudly displayed in the Cunningham home is this scroll giving Larry the freedom of Boston presented during the heyday of his success among the Irish in America in 1982.

RTÉ'S RONAN WAS THERE: A bearded Ronan Collins (first on left) at the launch of Larry's K-Tel album with the late Peter Sheridan, manager of Larry, a K-Tel staff member, Beatrice and Larry Cunningham.

BIBI AND FRIENDS: RTÉ'S BiBi Baskin with the late Joe Dolan, former Taoiseach Albert Reynolds and Larry on the set of one of her TV shows.

COOL LARRY: The songs of Larry were still cool in 1983 according to the *Evening Press*.

COUNTRY BOY: Larry is described as one of Longford's most well-known people by the *Longford Leader*.

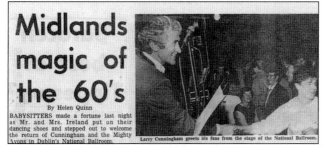

DUBLIN COMEBACK: Huge crowds attend the first comeback dance by Larry and the original Mighty Avons.

COMBACK BOY: Larry and the original Mighty Avons on their highly successful comeback tour in 1986. Front row: Jimmy and Peter Smith and Larry. Back row: Gerry Walshe, Paddy Smith and Brian Finlay (all three since deceased). Ronnie Griffiths and Micky Brady.

SHIP SHAPE: Larry in a promotional photo for the B&I line.

CRUISE STARS: Larry with other entertainers pictured on a cruise ship. On either side of him at the back are Liam Clancy and the late Tommy Makem. Also in the back row (second from right) is the late Dermot O'Brien. Front extreme right is comedian Hal Roach.

COUNTRY PRIDE: Larry on tour with American Country star Charley Pride.

UK AWARDS: At an Irish World awards ceremony in London with RTÉ TV Sports presenter Colm Murray.

LONGFORD ASSOCIATION IN DUBLIN 1954 - 2004

One of the giants of the Irish entertainment business, it was only right and fitting that Larry Cunningham should have been named as the Longford Person of the Year by the Dublin Assoc in 1988. As Leader reporter, Sheila Reilly, has been finding out, the award meant a huge amount to the Granard born entertainer and he has always retained a great fondness and high regard for the Dublin Assoc.

Assoc's stamp of approval raised our Larry's profile

LONGFORD PERSON OF THE YEAR: Larry is honoured by the Longford Association in Dublin in 2004.

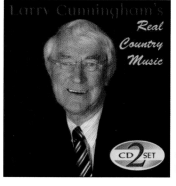

LARRY AND BIG THREE AT ÁRAS: Joe McCarthy of the Dixies, Paddy Cole, Sonny Knowles and Larry at Áras an Uachtaráin in 2001.

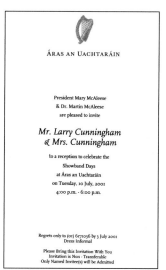

ÁRAS AN UACHTARÁIN

President Mary McAleese
& Dr. Martin McAleese
are pleased to invite

*Mr. Larry Cunningham
& Mrs. Cunningham*

to a reception to celebrate the
Showband Days
at Áras an Uachtaráin
on Tuesday, 10 July, 2001
4:00 p.m. - 6:00 p.m.

Regrets only to (01) 6171036 by 3 July 2001
Dress Informal

Please Bring this Invitation With You
Invitation is Non - Transferable
Only Named Invitee(s) will be Admitted

INVITATION: Larry and Beatrice are very proud of their invitation to Áras an Uachtaráin.

LARRY'S LATEST: A recently released double CD on the Ceol label featuring some of Larry's biggest hits recorded in Nashville.

TOGETHER: Larry and Beatrice.

FAMILY TIME: Larry and Beatrice with their children in Spring 2009. Back row: Sinéad, Lorcán, Barry and Regina.

SHOWBAND DEGREE! When Larry's son Barry got his degree at Dublin City University in 2005, his mother Beatrice identified a nice photo opportunity for father and son beside a poster advertising the Showband show which Larry was a guest on at that time.

GRANDCHILDREN: Peter and Molly Sheridan.

remembers that he thought on that night it was as big as the town of Granard!

'We enjoyed every minute of it and believe it or not I was not very nervous as I had the lads with me. I was not there on my own and there were eight of us out there on stage together. Concerts at that time were not frequent gigs for us; it was showband dances almost all of the time. To sit on stage on your own and perform out there in front of the band to a sit-down audience could be frightening,' admits Larry.

He agrees that as they were not familiar with playing to sit-down audiences, it was something that he was 'a little uneasy about' for the first few songs. He did his best to enjoy doing this sort of show and put on the best possible performance for the crowd.

Larry also recalls that this was a very different music programme to what the band would be doing in the ballrooms back home. The New York crowd had not come to hear the pop songs of that era. They wanted the Irish and country material that he would be performing.

'I knew that I would be singing 75 per cent of Irish material and the remaining 25 per cent would be Jim Reeves' songs.' He thinks that he sang for 'about an hour' and the other acts on stage that night did about 'an hour and a half' in total.

He gives the impression that he didn't do much market research in advance regarding the sort of show that would go down best with the audience at Carnegie Hall. But he was aware of how Carmel Quinn had wooed the audiences there annually for many years.

It was in the mid 1950s that Dublin-native Carmel Quinn went to America. This was after a spell of working with bands and orchestras in Ireland and the UK. She quickly got a spot on the popular Arthur Godfrey *Talent Scouts* shows in the US.

The New York Daily News dated 15 March 1998, had this to say about the early career of Quinn in the land of her adoption. 'She was quite the find when popular television was growing from 10-inch screens to those great big 12-inchers.'

Quinn is quoted in the story. She says that after she won a prize of three mornings on the Godfrey show Arthur asked her to join and she stayed for six years

'Talk about luck, I didn't know it was such a big show. I hadn't been further than Newark. And, anyway, back in Ireland television wasn't such a big deal. Ignorance is bliss,' stated Quinn. She was then Mrs Fuller (the couple later divorced) when Larry Cunningham replaced her for his one St Patrick's Night concert in Carnegie Hall.

Audiences in America came to know and love Carmel's style of singing. They also liked the way she would tell humorous tales about life back home in the Emerald Isle.

'Ever since then, (when she arrived in the USA) Carmel Quinn has been as much associated with St Patrick's Day as are corned beef and cabbage,' states the story in *The New York Daily News*.

Larry Cunningham corroborates that story. 'Carmel was

always talking about baking the bread and making porridge back home. She made a fortune talking about this and singing songs that tied-in with such scenes.'

Larry adds, 'we knew that she also made a point of going to the front door after each show to shake hands with members of the audience. Bill Fuller asked me and the late Tommy Makem to do likewise.'

He also remembers the scene afterwards when Bill Fuller asked himself and Tommy Makem to go to the Green Room. Larry laughs about this as he says there was a rip-roaring party going on there. But he could not partake in the drinking, as he was a member of the Pioneer Total Abstinence Association at the time.

With a smile he remembers that some of the seven lads in the Mighty Avons who were on stage with him were not Pioneers. They enjoyed themselves in the Green Room afterwards!

Larry – In Exhalted Company

It seems that Larry was unfazed by the fact that The Beatles, Harry Belafonte, Benny Goodman, Judy Garland and many other international stars had played in this hallowed hall.

According to the website www.carnegiehall.org Bill Haley and the Comets (of 'Rock Around the Clock' fame) were the first rock 'n' roll band to appear there in 1955. No other similar act appeared there until 12 February 1964. That was when The Beatles performed two shows there during their first trip to the United States.

But some US country acts were there before Larry Cunningham and the Mighty Avons. They may have done original versions of songs that Larry and the lads covered at Carnegie Hall on their first appearance there.

According to the book *Nashville's Grand Ole Opry* by Jack Hurst (Abrams New York 1975), American country stars first played Carnegie Hall in the late 1940s. 'Two performances in Carnegie Hall on consecutive nights in the autumn of 1947 were solid successes.

'Ernest Tubb headlined these first Opry forays into the nation's best-known concert hall. He was accompanied by Minnie Pearl, Dot and Smokey Swann and some other acts from the East,' states Hurst. The story documents some early attempts by country music stars to make inroads into the scene in New York.

Minnie Pearl is quoted in the same book as saying that there was not much press coverage of the shows. But they were reviewed, and 'panned' in *Variety* magazine which did not impress her! (Nashvilles Grand Ole Opry, p.140)

However in 1961 she returned to the same stage. This time the singer that Larry Cunningham came to idolise, Jim Reeves, was also on the show. Others on that night included Patsy Cline, Marty Robbins, Bill Monroe, Faron Young and Grandpa

Jones. The legendary Jordanaires, who often worked as backing vocalists with Elvis Presley, were there too.

But, unlike Larry Cunningham, America's Grand Ole Opry star Minnie Pearl did not feel comfortable performing on stage at Carnegie Hall. Her stage routine included a lot of comedy as well as singing and it seems that the comedy may have failed to impress the New York audiences.

'Most comedy must be done slowly to be effective. When I'm nervous about a show I tend to go too fast. I was that way at Carnegie Hall every time. I got off wrong in my timing. Carnegie Hall overawed me,' said Minnie. (Nashvilles Grand Ole Opry, p. 296).

An Old Concert Poster

We do not have the benefit of any reviews from newspapers or books regarding the first appearance of Larry Cunningham and the Mighty Avons at Carnegie Hall. But even today, as far as the singer is concerned, it was never a big deal playing there or in any other hall, big or small.

'Back in Ireland my aim in my younger days was to work as a carpenter. Getting a qualification to teach woodwork was my big aim. I always wanted to work with my hands and not with my voice. So the last thing I thought about was being on any stage, anywhere, making a living as a singer.

'So when I went on to playing in the small halls here in Ireland at first it was no big deal. When the Carnegie Hall gig came along it was a great honour to do it but it was just another different gig. We were back in a ballroom in Castlerea or some other Irish town again and playing to two or three thousand dancers a few weeks later. At that time the New York gig did not seem to mean very much to the fans,' he adds. Larry also says there was not much media coverage in Ireland in the mid-1960s regarding his appearance in Carnegie Hall. He attributes this to lesser interest by the regional press in shows by Irish artists so far away from the homeland. At that time there were no local radio stations in Ireland and Radio Éireann was the dominant broadcaster.

But Larry has vivid memories about the show itself and the controversy regarding the circuitous way that he came to be informed of the date. However his recall regarding the plane journey to and from the USA at the time is very sketchy. He says all he remembers is that the journey was much slower than similar flights today. Much of the delay was due to the plane making stops both in Dublin and Shannon.

In recent years Larry's memories of the Carnegie Hall gigs were reactivated when his daughter Sinéad visited New York. While on a visit to the famous venue she enquired of some people there about her father playing on its famous stage back in the 1960s.

A receptionist at Carnegie Hall told her that she might be able to trace details of the concert if she knew what year it happened. Larry's daughter telephoned home to find out what year he first played in Carnegie Hall. But when he got her telephone call he says he could not remember the year of the show. However after much searching the person Sinéad Cunningham was dealing with in Carnegie Hall located a poster for the concert. Not alone did she get a copy of it but she also got a copy of another poster for a show performed by Larry's idol Jim Reeves at this world-famous venue. It had happened a few years before the Longford man graced the same stage.

More US Concerts and Venues

After that first foray into the concert scene across the Atlantic, Larry and the band played many other venues in the USA. These included the Lincoln Centre and the City Hall in New York. He even recorded a live album with popular Irish radio and TV personality Jimmy Magee as MC at the latter show.

Larry says it was during the time that he was managed by Mick Clerkin (later Daniel O'Donnell's record label chief) that he played the Lincoln Centre. But it seems that the singer was dubious about attracting a capacity crowd to such a large venue.

He says they were lucky to have been able to secure the top international traditional Irish music group the Chieftains to work with them on that show. The mix of folk, traditional and country 'n' Irish obviously helped swell the audience numbers.

Larry's wife, Beatrice, was in the audience that night. She was amazed at the reaction of so many of the Irish emigrants present when he came out to sing. He started off as usual with 'Come Back Home to Erin' which had an instant impact on the crowd.

Larry says that his wife told him afterwards that all she could see was a sea of white hankies. But they were not waving them in the air. Instead many of the audience beside her were drying their tears when they heard that song.

'My sister was there too and her remarks meant a lot to me afterwards. She was frank in her reaction to this scene regarding so many being emotional. She said if we were over there as long as some of those emigrants were, and not had the money to go home, we would be crying too.'

During this appearance by Larry at the Lincoln Centre and at his second concert at Carnegie Hall he was more confident. Those shows were some years after his first St Patrick's Night show at the prestigious New York concert hall. Larry says that all those concerts in the United States meant a lot both to him and to the musicians who worked with him.

He leans across the table as we sit in the foyer of The Longford Arms Hotel, talking enthusiastically about these concerts. But in particular it is the memory of the first one in Carnegie Hall from those days of yesteryear that Larry still relishes most of all.

'Carnegie Hall was one of a number of highs for me in the

States and that first night there is one high that I'll never forget. We did it again; I played Carnegie Hall a second time for Bill Fuller. It was not because Carmel was pregnant again but due to him being so pleased with how we got on at the first show there. He enjoyed it immensely and said we would be doing a similar show again at the same venue but not on a St Patrick's Night,' Larry enthuses.

These remarks are interesting coming from such a discerning, and sometimes such a controversial promoter. Apparently Bill Fuller was impressed enough by Larry Cunningham's performance to invite him to play Carnegie Hall again. That's most telling coming from a man who does not seem to have been a big fan of the King of Rock 'n' Roll, the late Elvis Presley.

An obituary published in *The Guardian* newspaper in the UK on Tuesday 9 September 2008 gives some insight into his views on Elvis. According to the writer, Ann Scanlon, the promoter had built up an empire of entertainment venues and hotels in Ireland and the UK before doing likewise in the USA. He is also attributed with getting The Royal Showband to play dates in Las Vegas as far back as 1966.

This obituary quotes Fuller's friend, Frank Murray, who went on to manage the Electric Ballroom and Fuller's favourite band The Pogues. It claims that he remembers Bill telling him that somebody once offered to introduce him to Elvis Presley. To this Bill Fuller is reported to have said, 'F . . k Elvis, I want to meet the Colonel!'

It seems that his interest in contacting Colonel Tom

Parker, the manager of Elvis, was greater than any desire he had to meet the star himself!

However Fuller reversed the roles on the day he telephoned a rural post office in County Longford. He bypassed management to directly book Irish Country King Larry Cunningham to play one of the most memorable dates of his career – in Carnegie Hall.

Seven
A Rambling Irishman

They were a wild but not a wicked lot, Irish teenagers of the 1960s who were emigrants in strange lands. For some, Elvis Presley was the 'King' of Rock 'n' Roll, for others Larry Cunningham was the 'King' of Country 'n' Irish. To this day it is obvious from his expressions that Larry hated that royal title. Indeed later on in Larry's career he spurned a chance to see the King of Rock 'n' Roll in action. Dismissively Larry said he could see Elvis another day, but death decided differently.

As he and Elvis ploughed different musical furrows in the 1960s, Irish teenagers flocked in thousands to ballrooms far from their homeland to see Larry and other Irish stars. Those young Irish emigrants had, albeit unwillingly, abandoned their earlier accommodation, mostly in whitewashed thatched homes, for new abodes in dingy digs in Camden, The Bronx or Boston. To say they 'flocked' to the ballrooms abroad is almost an understatement. They flocked like sheep into many such venues; a never-to-be-broken record crowd of 6,850 saw Larry and the band at one London-Irish ballroom in 1966.

'There was a multitude of these dancehalls in Britain, and perhaps the best-known of all was The Galtymore in Cricklewood. It had two separate halls – a Céilídh Hall and a Modern Dancing Hall.' (*The Men Who Built Britain* by Ultan Cowley – Wolfhound Press 2001, p.216).

'Thousands had Come to See Us'

In 1966, a year before Larry's record-breaking and record-making Galtymore gig, the 'Tribute to Jim Reeves' was a hit in Britain. This hit gave Larry and his band a chance to tour the bigger Irish ballroom circuit. He says that for a year after his debut record the crowds were steadily building in the Irish ballrooms across Britain.

But Larry and the band were still not commanding huge fees until after 'Lovely Leitrim' – when everything was changed, utterly changed. As was the practice with many bands at that time, their management sought and secured bookings for UK and USA tours up to a year in advance.

'My manager, Charlie McBrien, booked this particular tour long before "Lovely Leitrim" became a hit. Among the dates were a few in the ballrooms operated by the Burns organisation in England, including The Galtymore in London. By the time we got there "Leitrim" had been a hit but the agreed fee before all this happened was £250. However when The Galtymore gig came around the band was earning four times that figure,' he remembers. This 'agreed fee' was to leave an aggrieved Larry licking his wounded financial feelings after he created a never-to-be-broken record for a London-Irish ballroom gig.

Larry can only imagine how much money was taken in on the door alone that night (possibly £3,425) plus all that accrued from sales of minerals, teas, snacks etc. This was not a typical dance attendance for a touring Irish band. This crowd was phenomenal for Larry and the lads who were probably still weary after the long journey by boat and road from Longford to London. At that time a typical tour of ballrooms in the UK started with a less than luxurious sea trip to Holyhead or Liverpool, sometimes on a boat also taking a cargo of cattle! As far as Larry can remember the record-breaking crowd at The Galtymore was at the start of that British tour for the band.

'I believe that it was at the start as I wasn't prepared for what happened. But as the rest of the tour went on each ballroom that we played in was breaking its own crowd records. Of course none of the crowds were as big as the attendance at The Galtymore as none of the other halls were big enough to hold that sort of crowd. The Gresham, The National and The Buffalo were big – but not as big as The Galtymore.'

But at the start of that momentous evening's entertainment Larry and the lads were blissfully unaware of the commotion they would cause in Cricklewood.

'I remember distinctly arriving at the small dressing room upstairs at The Galtymore that evening. You could look out one window and see down Cricklewood Road. But if you looked out another window you could see the Kilburn Road where it joined it. I thought I was seeing things when I looked up that way. All I could see were rows of people, two or three across each row. They were all backed up out of sight which meant the queue was at least over a mile long. The last thing I expected was that all these people were coming to see me.

'Then when some of the other members of the band arrived in, they said that as they were coming in they had great difficulty getting through the crowds milling outside. They added that there was pandemonium outside with people trying to get in. The next thing we heard was that the ballroom which was adjoining the main one, the Céilí Hall, was also being opened and the crowds were being allowed to spill into both halls. It transpired that even before we took to the stage both ballrooms were full.

'Suddenly the realisation hit me for the first time ever that these thousands had come to see us. Indeed up to then I had not taken this showbusiness thing too seriously. I thought it was one of those things that had happened for us and it could end at any time. If it stopped I wasn't worried either as my trade meant more to me up to then,' he recalls.

Hurtful Heavy-Handed Tactics

The usual procedure was that Larry and the band would arrive on stage together and their first tune would be 'Come Back Home to Erin'.

'But I remember on that night about five minutes before we were due on stage we looked out and people were packed in everywhere. They stood or sat on the steps of the stairways, the sides of the stage, all the little nooks and crannies were full of fans. The stairs which the band used to get to the stage was so packed with people that we could see no way through the crowd. It seems that anyone who could get any place to stand did so and they did not, or could not, move from where they were.

'Suddenly the dressing room door opened and two bouncers entered. They said something like "Lads, it's time to get out there" and we all stood up to do so. But they turned to me and said that I would not be going out then. They said they would come up for me later. As this had never happened to me before I said to them that I could make my way down there by myself anyway. But they said "No!" to that and as they were both about six foot six inches tall I did not argue with them,' admits Larry.

But he still has critical views of some of the actions of the bouncers during his record-breaking London gig. 'Bouncers played a big part in keeping things right in those ballrooms. But sometimes they also played a big part in situations going wrong. On occasions they did not do what they were supposed to do properly. That night, after the band had started playing, the bouncers came back to bring me down. That is one experience that I will never forget as I was very unhappy about the way they got me through the crowd.

'There were wee lassies there that I knew and they were just pushed aside. You could say they were manhandled and abused by those who were taking me through. It was something that went through my heart as I helplessly watched this happening. They took me through the Céilí Hall first. But by the time I got to the stage and had to watch these bouncers manhandling fans all around me I was livid . . . I was raging.

'When I got to the back entrance of the stage I said to the bouncers, 'Now boys ye have the job done! Please get out of my way and I never want to see anything like this happen again and it won't – if I can avoid it!'

Money Matters

Larry continues, 'When I got to the microphone and looked down at the crowd it was just a sea of heads. You could not see a floorboard anywhere. I don't believe that anyone could have danced as they were so tightly packed together. But even then it never dawned on me how many thousands might be there.

'It was only afterwards I was told that the attendance was 6,850. Yet we were still only given our fee of £250 and I was really annoyed. But because that was the contract, that was what was written on paper, we didn't get any more. Why wouldn't I be annoyed? The dance attracted 6,850 and as far as I remember it was also one of the first times they charged a ten shillings (50 pence) entrance fee? Of course the Burns organisation were within their rights as the fee of £250 was what was written in the contract. But I said the next time we would play there things would be different and they were,' Larry states emphatically

All this adulation and the screaming packed crowd was not something that Larry was familiar with either. 'When I saw what I had to go through that night, I said if this is what's going to be happening in the future I'm not going to be part of it. If that is all one gets for being nearly half killed, I said I'm not going back there again. Indeed I was so upset about many aspects of that night that I said I might not even bother with showbusiness again.

'When that news went back to the head office of the Burns organisation in London the whole scene changed for us. Afterwards I think they were sorry that they had not been more flexible with our fee that night. But in fairness to them they were very good to us over the years since then and I played their ballrooms for decades. Indeed I was playing at The Galtymore up to a few years ago and still getting good crowds there,' he adds.

Michael Burns, manager of The Galtymore Ballroom, had his own views on Larry's status among the Irish emigrants. 'In the 1960s with the emigration from Ireland there were a lot of

Irish people here away from home. They came to The Galtymore to meet up, socialise and find out about what was going on at home – the news and the gossip. When singers such as Larry Cunningham came to London from home they were looked upon, and were in their time, the superstars. Larry Cunningham was a superstar and he holds the record for the biggest crowd here at The Galtymore. It was the time of "Lovely Leitrim" and during the Jim Reeves' era when Larry Cunningham was Ireland's version [of Jim Reeves].' (Paschal Mooney *Irish Music Legends* RTÉ Radio 5 January 2006).

By 1969 Larry was dividing his time between ballrooms in Ireland, Britain and the USA. He was still packing The Galtymore and now had moved up to play at the first International Festival of Country Music at nearby Wembley. Larry was all over the place and so it was appropriate to title his album, released that summer, *A Ramblin' Irishman*. Appropriately too he was pictured on the cover with seven Aer Lingus hostesses beside a plane ready for take-off to some dance somewhere in the UK or USA.

Love 'n' Lust in the Ballrooms

Even after splitting with the Mighty Avons in 1969 Larry continued to play for the Burns organisation at ballrooms in Manchester and London. He also worked for many other Irish dancing promoters all over the UK.

Larry has many memories of the Gresham in Holloway Road, London that had a revolving stage and where he played with both the Avons and the Country Blue Boys.

'I remember during the time when "Lovely Leitrim" was a hit, the crowd outside it was so big that they broke the glass doors trying to get in.' But were the Irish ballrooms in the UK as rough as they were reputed to be? Larry has his own observations on that. 'In a lot of cases this rough image was exaggerated. You must remember that this was in the 1960s and people were not long over in England. They had a few pounds in their pockets that they never had at home and they might also have an extra few pints before going dancing.'

To some extent this observation is mild compared to the views of emigrant Joe McGarry in *The Men Who Built Britain*. 'I was goin' across (the hall) and no one would dance with me because I was mad drunk. I was saying, "What the f . . k is wrong with me? I'm young, and I've got a three-piece suit on, and I've got a few bob in my pocket – what the f . . k's going on?" And of course the answer was, I was totally drunk.' (*The Men Who Built Britain*, p.214).

In the same book a matron in a British hospital is quoted as warning trainee nurses to be wary of the Irish navvies. 'Have nothing to do with those Irish navvies, girls. It's just the grace of God that keeps their trousers up!' But lines quoted from another book by author Ultan Cowley are very much at variance with the unnamed hospital matron, 'The Irish navvies were very devout; many prayed openly night and morning and displayed religious pictures in their lockers; all of them attended Mass on Sundays'. (*Navvies: Their Social Relations*, Sociology 3, Sykes, A.J.M. – 1969, p.161).

Who was right and who was wrong? Even though he was an emigrant worker for a short period during the 1950s Larry Cunningham's contact with the grassroots London-Irish scene in the 1960s was more remote. His was more a peripheral association then. As a singing star on stage he was shielded from many rowdy ballroom scenes, which were quickly quelled by bouncers. According to Ultan Cowley's book the men dressed well when going to dances at the Irish ballrooms in London. He says the men dressed in a navy blue suit with a white shirt and a blue or red tie. 'In the Gresham (ballroom) as elsewhere, a tie could be rented for a shilling at the door prior to admission.' (*The Men Who Built Britain*, p.214).

When asked about this Larry Cunningham seemed surprised and said he was unaware that some emigrants rented ties at the doors of dancehalls. These were some of the people who helped make him a star in the UK as Eugene McGloin wrote. 'Many emigrants were disgracefully forced out of here in the 1950s. They became the actual people who bought the records which made Larry Cunningham the first-ever Irish-based artiste to break into the British charts.' (*The Longford News* 6 September 1985).

Many marriages were made as a result of courtships which started in the Irish ballrooms of London or Manchester and other places where the Irish emigrants were. The Buffalo in Camden Town was a hotspot for Irish love or lust according to emigrant Liam Walsh. It was also one of the Bill Fuller ballrooms that Larry Cunningham regularly played in.

'If you wanted to be sure of getting "a claim" for the night you went to The Buffalo. It was said that if a man (any man) couldn't get a woman in The Buffalo the best thing he could do was – lie down and die!' (*The Men Who Built Britain,* p.216).

Spawning Oasis

Larry also played one of Bill Fuller's ballrooms in Manchester, the Astoria on Plymouth Grove. It was here that Peggy Sweeney met another Irish emigrant, Thomas Gallagher, in 1964.

A quarter of a century later, on 29 May 1989 Noel Gallagher returned to the ballroom where his parents first laid eyes on each other to celebrate his 21st birthday. By this time, Fuller, who still owned the building, had changed its name to The Carousel and, more recently, the International 2. Noel Gallagher was there to see The Stone Roses who were supporting James at an Anti-Clause 28 Benefit gig and he was blown away.

'The Stone Roses made me want to be in a band', he says. (electric-ballroom.co.uk/history) The same internet page on the life and times of Bill Fuller also states that Liam Gallagher saw Ian Brown perform for the first time that night and it was a Damascene moment. 'I thought it's here, today, in my face. I can go with that.'

So an Irish ballroom in Manchester helped spawn Oasis even though the Gallaghers, parents or sons, may not have been at Larry Cunningham's dances! However, during many of Larry's tours this Manchester ballroom would be the last one on the trip before heading for the boat back home from Holyhead. Many of the tours were during Lent when Larry says many bands could manage a three-week tour of venues in Britain and four weeks in the States. This filled up the diary nicely for the seven weeks of Lent when there would be no dancing at home.

'I remember often sailing over and back on a cattle boat named *The Princess Maud*. During the start of Lent it would be packed with bands. The situation was the same in the weeks before Christmas and I remember buying a lovely topcoat on one occasion before I returned home for Christmas. A man was lucky to be able to afford a topcoat back then. The one that I bought in England was a gabardine coat which was the popular type at the time. Anyway on the way home the boat started to rock and the heat down below deck was unbearable. I took off my new topcoat and left it beside my case in a corner and went upstairs to get some fresh air, as I was feeling sick. While I was away it seems that a few people had been lying on my coat and you should see the state of it. Some of them had got sick all over it. So that was the end of my topcoat – it never made it back to Longford,' he remembers with a laugh.

Avoiding the Parties

Touring in the US resulted in some boring moments for Larry and his fellow musicians and managers. As they only played at weekends they had very little to do from Monday to Friday.

'We flew from one city to another and the gear was also taken by plane. The general trend was that we played Friday, Saturday and Sunday in New York, mostly for Bill Fuller. Those gigs were usually in the City Centre Ballroom and it would be packed. I'm talking of crowds close to 3,000 people each night. You would be bored stiff from then until the following weekend when you would play for three nights in an Irish ballroom in Boston. Then it was on to Chicago or Los Angles for the following Friday, Saturday and Sunday before you came back to New York for the final weekend. That would be back in the City Centre Ballroom and the crowds again would be as big as when the tour started.'

He admits that there were times when they had small crowds along the way too. 'But I don't remember any gig where the crowd was so small that we did not get to play. If that ever happened then I don't remember it or I don't want to remember it,' he exclaims. 'But there were times when we would be booked by promoters abroad for 12 gigs and you would have six or seven great ones. Then you would find yourself put into a gig that was a comedown and a shame to be a part of it, especially in front of an emigrant audience. I'm talking about both England and America. But if you met a promoter like that your aim was not to work for him again. If you let it happen a second time it was your fault.'

RTÉ's Jimmy Magee says he witnessed some memorable moments with Larry in the USA. 'A standing ovation in San Francisco . . . eight curtain calls in Philadelphia. I've seen and heard it all,' he wrote in the sleeve notes for the album *Best of Larry Cunningham in Concert*. This album was recorded live before 4,000 fans at The Lincoln Centre, New York. Jimmy states the welcome there was deafening and they would have waited all night listening to Larry. Only for the regulations by either 'the New York Fire Department or the staff union at the Centre that it had to be vacated by 11.30 p.m.' they would have partied with him all night.

Larry says they could be attending parties with Irish emigrants every night if they had enough time while on tour in the States. 'But you had to draw the line somewhere as otherwise you would be up all night talking and perhaps taking a few drinks as well. So a lot of the offers of parties we refused. They were lovely people and while we would have loved to attend many of the parties our touring schedules often prevented this. However we got to visit a lot of people during the four days that we were off between touring each weekend in the USA.

Knife Attack in Chicago

Sometimes safety was a worry too for the touring Irish

musicians, especially in big cities such as Chicago. During one trip there Larry and another well-known Irish entertainer were told the address of the guesthouse they were staying in by Larry's manager. The manager was going there before the end of the show. But Larry and the other entertainer did not write down the address correctly and ended up in a dangerous part of town.

The taxi driver said he doubted that the address they gave him was correct but on their insistence he took them there. He was right. No such house number existed on the street where they stopped off. It was in the early hours of the morning and the area looked mean, real mean. They stopped at a filling station and Larry's friend got out to seek directions. He was immediately surrounded by a bunch of thugs and as one of them drew a knife he barely made it back into the taxi uninjured. 'It was so close that the thug slit the side of the leg of his pants as he jumped back into the taxi and we sped away. The driver went to a police station and we eventually got proper directions to our destination on the other side of town. It was a worrying time,' admits Larry.

Not the Best of Times Nor the Worst of Times

Beatrice Cunningham says she also worried a little more when Larry was on tour in the USA especially when their children were still small. 'You always felt he was so much further away than when touring in England. If something went wrong at home he could be back from England quickly but at that time

America was such a long journey. He might be over as far as California, San Francisco and Los Angeles which were places another world away.

But you got on with your daily life and the business kept me busy. I had great support also from my own family and from Larry's family. His mother, Lord rest her, was always there in those times as was my sister-in-law Rose and his brother Michael who was a great support to me. They lived close by so I saw them every day. My own late father and mother were only three miles away and if I was in major difficulty I could leave off a baby with some one of them and they would mind the child,' recalls Beatrice.

The wife of American country star George Hamilton IV, Tinky Hamilton, once said that the years his career was at its peak were the best and the worst years. No amount of prompting, probing or questioning would make Beatrice speak out in similar tones about Larry's tours abroad while at the peak of his popularity. 'I suppose it was a difficult time but we both knew we had jobs to do. It was his career, his life and his way of making a good living for us all. He was a great support for all the family – so having said that we coped. We did not dwell too much on it. Being so busy during the day when night came I was too tired to think too much about it and that is how I handled it really. At the time I thought I was killed trying to keep up with all that was going on. But looking back now they were lovely times.'

She says she had the enjoyment of the children but she often felt sorry for Larry because he missed out on that. 'But now he is having a second run with our two beautiful grandchildren Molly and Peter. I can look at him now and see how much he is enjoying them as they grow up and he is a big part of their life which is great,' she adds. She doesn't think their children missed out that much as they were all into football, swimming etc. But one problem was that Larry would bring back too many treats for them from wherever he was on tour.

'With birthdays and Christmas and all that we had to cut down a bit and leave some stuff in the attic for another day. Sometimes I would have to meet him up the road and say not to show them all the stuff he had brought back that day. As I was trying to discipline them I felt at times that I was too hard on them and Daddy was too good to them. But we sorted it out as best we could and kept an even balance most of the time.'

Beatrice and Larry are grateful that they were all well-grounded children and caused them no bother. 'It was a simpler time in Ireland as they did not have all the electronic things that they have today. Lego was a huge thing with our two boys and when Larry would bring them back Lego they loved working with it. The next time he was away they might have a plane or a boat made and they would say that their Dad was off travelling on that. I see that Lego is making a comeback now and I am delighted. I feel that it helps sharpen children's minds which is of benefit to them at school as well,' suggests Beatrice.

Barriers to Stop Singers Falling off Stages!

Larry and the band, and many touring Irish bands, came back home from tours with other links for families of emigrants as well as presents for their own children. These other links were requests from the USA in an era long before e-mail, the internet or mobile phones.

'We would bring bundles of requests back home for playing at dances in different parts of the country. Members of their families would attend our dances hoping to hear a request from their loved ones given to us while we were in the States. The emigrants might have written home before we arrived back to tell their families that we would be playing requests for them in their local ballroom the next time we appeared there.' This was mostly during his early USA tours with the Mighty Avons when links with home were more difficult for the Irish in the US.

It was many years later when Larry did his longest-ever tour in the USA with Mayo-born entertainer Noel Henry and his band. Larry remembers, 'He had an excellent band and he wanted to do the longest tour ever by an Irish music show in the States. I remember him phoning me and saying that he wanted me to work with him on the tour which would require us playing shows in 26 states. He phoned me a year and a half in advance and my reply was that I could be dead by then! Anyway I agreed and also on the tour was one of my band, Billy Faughnan from Mohill, Sean Dunphy, ballad singer Mary McGonigle and comedian Noel V Ginnity. Noel Henry and his band were as big an attraction as any of us at all the venues and we did the dates in 26 states in 30 days.

'We spent a lot of time at airports and we got much of our sleep on planes. When he sent me the brochure in advance of the tour I rang him and said I was going to frame it if it was a success. I had worked with different acts over the years and usually half of the tour would be fine and the other half would be full of problems. But I had to frame this one because everything worked. It was so well planned that most Saturday nights we would be staying close to a church so we had no excuse for not getting Mass either that evening of the next morning. We played places that I never played before or since. Those included Tampa in Florida and San Antonio, Texas.

'The four days that we had for relaxing he planned them so we would be able to do some sight-seeing. After the San Antonio gig he took us to The Alamo the next day. There were doubts in my mind about anyone turning up at Tampa in Florida at 3.30 in the afternoon. I remember Noel V Ginnity looking out before we went on stage and he said it was packed. But he said they were not a crowd of screaming fans.

'When I looked out from behind the curtain I agreed. It was like a sea of cotton with all the fans having white heads like myself,' laughs Larry. He has a humorous observation too about the barriers in front of the stages of many modern ballrooms both at home and abroad.

'Nearly every ballroom in Ireland, England and America in the 1960s had some sort of rail or barrier across the front of the stage. Only a few years ago Brendan Bowyer and myself were doing a 33-date tour at home and I remember one venue in Navan which had a beautiful brass railing around the stage. I decided to tell the crowd what I was thinking about, as I was half way through my part of the show. I said that years ago the railings were put around ballroom stages to keep women from pulling their favourite singers off the stage. Sez I to the crowd, today these barriers are used to prevent singers of my age from falling off the stage!'

'We Can See That *garsún* Elvis Another Time'

Memories keep flooding back for Larry of times spent on tour abroad – some happy, others sad or humorous. But one that he remembers best of all is when he turned down the chance to see Elvis in action in Las Vegas.

'We had finished playing on a Sunday night in Chicago and we knew that we would be twiddling our thumbs for the following four days. At that time Brendan Bowyer, Tom Dunphy and The Royal showband were working in Las Vegas. We rang Tom and of course he was delighted that we were over. He told us to take the first flight to Las Vegas. Unlike on Aer Lingus flights where you got a sweet to chew to prevent your ears popping, we got packs of playing cards on that flight to Vegas,' he laughs.

But Larry and many on board had more to worry about than playing cards when they hit a pocket of turbulence on that flight. There were three of them in each row of seats. The man sitting beside Larry's manager Mick Clerkin and himself stayed playing a card game throughout the terrifying turbulence experience.

'We were about an hour into the flight when in my opinion the plane started to turn upside down. It was unbelievable and I thought it was the end of the line. Mick Clerkin's face was as white as snow. This was even more noticeable as he had a head of jet-black hair at the time. Thank God I was never afraid on a plane before, and apart from that incident I've never been afraid since. Indeed when I saw the fellow beside us continuing playing his card game it helped calm me. I assumed that he had often experienced this sort of flying situation before.

'The pilot announced that he had moved up to a higher altitude to escape the turbulence. He said he understood that a plane underneath us had got into difficulties in a thunder and lightening storm but we had avoided that. When we arrived at our hotel room in Las Vegas and turned on the TV we discovered that the other plane had crashed. We were so exhausted that we headed for our beds and we had two beds in a hotel room that were each as big as a townland!

'The next day we went to see the show that Brendan Bowyer, Tom and the band were doing and it was brilliant. There were several other shows in Las Vegas that week and the one that I decided I would like to see was the Jimmy Dean show. He was the man who had a hit with 'Big John' many years earlier'.

But in the meantime Mick Clerkin had got tickets for a show that Elvis Presley was doing on that same night. One can only imagine this sort of scenario unfolding earlier that evening as Larry and Mick stood there on the sidewalk in sweltering Las Vegas.

They marvelled at their good fortune to have been gifted two sets of concert tickets for two very different stars – Elvis and Jimmy Dean – but alas – for concerts which were taking place on the same night.

As Larry and Mick deliberated about which concert to attend, there was a sudden buzz of excitement and noise along the sidewalk.

All eyes turned to the white stretch limo as it came cruising down the street.

There in the rear seat sat the 'King' with his trademark high rhinestone collar and dark glasses, smiling and waving to the onlookers as he sped past.

On his way to do a concert, no doubt.

Larry took another longer look at the two sets of tickets in his hand.

Which concert to go and see?

'Well Jimmy Dean is 42 years old and Elvis is only 35,' calculated Larry. 'I'm not so sure about Jimmy Dean but sure we can see that *garsún* (young fellow) Elvis another time,' he said to Mick. Larry's manager was not impressed as he was an Elvis fan and it could be another 10 years before they would be in Las Vegas again. 'But I had to keep my boss happy,' he recalls.

They went to see Jimmy Dean. Thirty-eight years later

Jimmy, who now lives in Richmond, Virginia, was still appearing in concerts. He performed at a show in Tennessee to mark his 80th birthday in 2008 and 'Big John' is still the highlight of his live performances.

His Las Vegas show attended by Larry and Mick all those decades ago was a great concert. 'It was a classy show, more 'middle of the road' music than country, and closer to what Dean Martin would do,' remembers Mick. It was the summer of 1970. They can only imagine what the competing concert given by Elvis that night was like

Well Larry never did get to see that *garsún* Elvis.

Elvis dropped dead suddenly in August 1977 at the age of 42.

Eight
No Sex or Drugs but All-Stars?

Some showband members, similar to those in some rock groups, were a promiscuous lot, or were they? Stories about that era suggest that sex was available almost on tap for the showband stars, up against the sagging sides of every carnival marquee! The groupies may also have been making love to the musicians under, and upon, kitchen tables in every sparsely furnished dancehall dressing room. But was it football, and not so much sex, sex and more sex, that was the main diversion for many singers? For some it seems that playing football and music for fundraising with the Jimmy Magee All-Stars on Monday nights was one diversion.

Both Larry Cunningham and top jazz player Paddy Cole have expressed views on the showband groupies ('autograph hunters') that seem to concur. When both made their views known, on very different forums, what they said was strangely similar. But others from the same showband scene, have talked and written about endless nights of sexual romps involving stars and fans.

It is difficult to winkle information out of Larry Cunningham about clandestine relationships that may have taken place between singers, musicians and fans. Drugs, irrespective of how minuscule, were part of the scene and it would be naive not to suggest that sex didn't also play a part. Larry accepts that there was some drug taking, though not so much on the country scene. He says the only drug that he took was tobacco as he was a cigarette smoker.

While reluctant to elaborate he does not deny that certain other improprieties went on. 'Ah! I know many singers had problems and almost everybody has skeletons in their cupboards in all walks of life. In the music business the biggest problem was to keep yourself as safe as possible,' claims Larry, who adds that an addiction to sport kept some of the singers safe and sane.

Using False Names

From the time that he was a child it seems Gaelic football was, and still is, an integral part of life for Larry. Indeed his association with the Jimmy Magee All-Stars seems to have dominated, much, though not all, of his leisure time during the halcyon era of the showbands. Before he recalls some days and nights with the All-Stars teams Larry turns the clock back even further. He talks enthusiastically of a time when his career as a minor footballer was taking off in tandem with his singing.

'My most memorable football game was a Longford minor championship final when I was playing with Granard and we were up against the Longford Slashers. We had met them earlier in the league and had beaten them. There was only a point between us as the championship final was in its closing stages. Suddenly a ball came in which could have drawn it for the Slashers. I went up and caught the ball and the trainer shouted at me as I fell down not to get up. We got a free out as I was on the ground and deemed to have been fouled and then the final whistle went and we were the champions.' Larry seems more excited recalling this moment that he is talking about his greatest music success.

He is less enthusiastic talking about any of the sex, drugs or other similar behind-the-scenes activities during the showband era. But start talking about football and words flow out of Larry's mouth like water from a tap.

'The year that we won the county championship I played minor for the Longford county team. We got as far as the Leinster semi-final but we lost. I blame the management,' he says.

'After playing at minor level here I went to England and ended up playing with a team in Derby named St Colman's. In those days the number of great footballers emigrating was amazing. But what was more amazing was the false names that they were playing under on teams abroad. This was for tax reasons and I worked with fellows for two years and I didn't know their real names until I was coming home,' laughs Larry. The last year he was in England, Larry's team faced 15 from Nottingham in the senior final of the emigrants' championship. 'It was a very rough game. You had tough, hardy, big men, many from Connemara who were much bigger than fellows such as me. But we had to face them. I was probably in good shape and I suppose my football skills were good enough too. Anyway we won the senior championship that year.'

After coming back home he played football on and off with local teams until he was almost 40. 'The only reason I gave it up then was due to the loss of sleep at weekends. Playing with the band so much and playing competitive club football on Sundays was a dangerous combination. Often when not fully rested after a Saturday night gig I would see two or three balls coming towards me in a club football game the next day! But of course I continued playing with the Jimmy Magee All-Stars and every game with them was a memorable game,' he adds.

Larry enthused about some of the greats that he played with from the inter-county football scene, many now gone to their eternal reward. 'God rest these greats such as Mattie McDonagh, Sean Purcell and Frank Stockwell from Galway and many more. We had a lot of fun playing on the Jimmy Magee All-Stars. I think two of the most memorable games I was involved in were played for a charity nominated by the great Mick O'Connell of Kerry. We played one of those in

Cork and the other on Valentia Island where he lived. I believe that everyone who was living on the island at the time was at the game. He was known as a man of few words who was more into football than talking. But we saw another side to him then after those games as he spoke so well and he was really well able to deal with people.'

Drinking All the Beer in Ballyjamesduff

The Jimmy Magee All-Stars started in Ballyjamesduff on the sixth of the sixth, sixty-six. 'All the sixes' according to the man responsible for the team, RTÉ broadcaster Jimmy Magee. 'I don't know who approached whom about the idea of a fundraising team of stars from showbands and sport. Larry Cunningham was one of those there at the early stages,' says Jimmy.

Larry has a vague recollection of how he became part of the All-Stars team. 'Jimmy was involved with our record promotional work at that time. Any day that he would be in the office we would be talking about sport. I think that at some stage he said to me that if we got a team together from the showbands he would get one from the RTÉ sports department and we would have a game. There were several others involved and he gathered up some of the football greats from the past while we helped get the showband players.' Larry added that the Mighty Avons and the Drifters showbands at the time could boast about 12 'class' footballers between them. So it was not too difficult to get that number up to 15 for a team. He thinks that Ballyjamesduff was chosen as a central venue for the first game as it was convenient for many of the showbands and Jimmy agrees with this.

Jimmy says it all really began with RTÉ's Bill O'Donovan and himself as well as anybody else who would listen to the silly sports dreams that he had!

'We would be talking about great football matches and ex-players and how we should put a team together. Nothing would do me until I went and organised the first All-Stars game. Showband manager Connie Lynch was very helpful. He came from Ballyjamesduff and he said he would help organise a game but I did not know if he was serious or not. Anyway I was serious and I invited a whole lot of fellows, including Larry who was a very important member of the first team. Others included Brendan Bowyer as well as the late Joe Dolan, Tom Dunphy and Doc Carroll. Another group included Mick Lynch and Frankie Byrne as well as many more lads from the world of sport,' remembers Jimmy. 'We went to Ballyjamesduff that very first evening and it was a massive success. But in the dressing room before the match, there was such a mix of musicians and sports stars that I was the only one there that knew everybody.'

According to Larry that first game went on much longer than the normal playing time of one hour. 'I would say that it probably lasted closer to two hours. There were so many lads that had to get a run, everybody wanted to be part of it and the field was packed with players. The concert afterwards in the Percy French Hotel was even bigger and the fans were outside and inside. They drank so much beer that night that they had to go to Cavan for extra supplies. All the beer in Ballyjamesduff was drunk before the morning light,' laughs Larry.

Friendly Game – Broken Jaw?

Jimmy agrees that the initial game and concert combination was a massive success. 'It was so successful that fellows were coming up to me afterwards saying that it was brilliant. Some were asking could we do this again? But what I hadn't told any of them was that I had arranged a whole season of games – 14 or 15 games were arranged for other Mondays during the rest of the year. For that first match we played a combination of players from the Mighty Avons and the Drifters and I wanted Larry to play on our team. But I think that he was recording or doing a TV show that day as he was late arriving. However, he arrived and played most of the match even though he wasn't there at the very start. Of course he played well and he played in countless other games with us afterwards.'

Even though he is listed as a sub on that first team in *The Swingin' Sixties* book, Jimmy says that it would be wrong to label Larry as a sub on the initial team. 'To say he was a sub would be downgrading him. As the current cross-channel soccer managers would say I was playing the rota system! Larry was one of our most regular players and he would be there for every match unless he was away in England or the USA on tour. His usual position was right full back and sometimes at full back. He could catch a ball well and kick it and of course he was a huge star on the music scene at that time.

'If you saw him playing you would know that he was enthusiastic. He would be out there jumping up and catching the ball with his knee up for protection, or for attacking, as he came down with the ball. It was his way of playing and not many fellows from the music scene were as lively as Larry in the early days. He knew what Gaelic football was all about. He realised that there could be somebody marking him at left corner forward who might have been an inter-county player at some time. Larry knew that his job was to make sure that his opponent did not get many kicks of the ball. If his opposite number did get the ball he would be harassing him to make sure that he did not score.'

Larry says that he took the games very seriously for the first few years. 'I think that even if my mother, God rest her, was on the pitch and playing against me I would not give her an easy time of it,' he claims. He also remembers one or two occasions when players from yesteryear tried to settle old scores when they met during the friendly games organised by the Jimmy Magee All-Stars.

'A small number of great players from yesteryear wanted to prove that they were still as good as during the high points of their careers. They wanted the crowd to see that they were still the best and you were liable to get a belt from them when going up for the ball. I won't forget one game when two great players from yesteryear were playing against each other, I can't mention names now, but one of them hit his opponent so hard that he suffered a suspected broken jaw. I was quoted afterwards as saying to the player responsible that we were raising funds to help people who were in wheelchairs. But we don't go out and behave in a manner that could put people in wheelchairs! However that did not happen again and Jimmy made sure that it did not,' he adds.

According to Larry, Jimmy operated his All-Stars games, and the concerts afterwards, very professionally. Fans would travel from one venue to another to see them play both on the field and on stage. 'There was football, charity, singing and music in it. It was a win win situation for everyone.'

Flying back from the USA to play . . . Football!

Larry remembers that members of Joe Dolan's band, The Drifters, were good players. He cites Tommy and Jimmy Swarbrigg, who later fronted their own band and sang in the Eurovision Song Contest, as great footballers from the showband scene.

Jimmy Magee agrees with this. 'There were a lot of good fellows around and certainly those two were among the top group of players. But Larry, and of course the late Dermot

O'Brien, were among the best Gaelic players from the showbands.' Nobody could deny Dermot O'Brien's Gaelic football pedigree as he had captained Louth to win the All-Ireland senior football final of 1957.

'The late Joe Dolan also played in many of those games.' But when asked if Joe was in the same league as Larry or Dermot O'Brien on the football field, Jimmy was hesitant in his answer. 'To be fair to Joe, now that he has passed away, I should say that he was a player like Maradonna. But that would be a lie. He was there for the fun and what fun we had and what a brilliant contributor Joe was at the concerts afterwards,' he remembers. A hit song from the showband era lists Larry and Joe Dolan as vital cogs in the Jimmy Magee All-Stars teams.

> *We had Cunningham and Dolan,*
> *They worked out a plan*
> *The pride of 'Lovely Leitrim' and 'The Jolly Tinkerman'.*
> *Says Larry, 'Joe you're a Drifter*
> *But I'll score one if it kills'*
> *The ball went through the net*
> *And landed in the 'Wicklow Hills'.*

> (The Hoedowners – McGregor/Hall
> – '*Showball Crazy*' 1966)

When asked if he had any input into writing the words for this song Jimmy Magee claims he was not involved. But he remembers it going to No 2 in the Irish Pop charts for The Hoedowners. He says Joe and Larry deserved to be mentioned in the song – Larry for his football skills in particular.

'As a footballer Larry Cunningham was there for the long haul. He was not just there on the first night. In fact he was there for many matches over the guts of 40 years. One night we were playing a charity match somewhere in England and I asked Larry if he would be available. He replied, "Look, a Mhic! I'll be there at some stage!" and he was,' laughs Jimmy.

Larry was playing a dance somewhere else in the UK. Towards the end of the concert that night there was still no sign of him and some of the boys said it was time to wrap it up. 'Larry was coming up from Liverpool and I said to the others that he had never let me down before. But I assumed that he could have been held up somewhere, as there might have been traffic delays or even an accident on the road that delayed him. I can't think of where we were; it may have been in Leeds or Birmingham but just as we were about to finish who should arrive but Larry. A show that was closing for the night reopened as Larry took to the stage.

'After he sang three or four songs the event took on a new lease of life and everybody just wanted it to go on and on. If Larry ever said that he would be there you could be sure that he would be there. That is one great trait in any man that he can stand by his word,' adds Jimmy.

Larry says most singers would make many sacrifices to support Jimmy Magee and the fundraising work carried out by his All-Stars. 'I remember playing a show in New York one

Sunday night and getting a flight home early the next day so that I would be back for a game. The flight I had to get was going to Belfast and I had somebody meeting me at the airport there to drive me to the game. It was in Navan that evening. But when we arrived at the pitch the gates were closed and the game was on. I had to throw my gear over the gate and then climb over it myself and run down to the dressing room to tog out. I remember that there was a Larry Smyth playing for Meath against us. He was at left corner forward and I was marking him. He told the story afterwards that every time we ran for the ball the crowd were shouting "get it Larry". But as we both had the same name neither of us knew who they were shouting for!'

'Lovely Leitrim' Played in Real Madrid!

Jimmy remembers that Larry travelled with them to play in Las Vegas and apart from being available so often for the teams over the years, they could also rely on him to play well in every match.

'Dressing rooms can be lonely places before matches if you are trying to get a team of good players together. Sometimes we might have seven or eight players togged out and then someone would say that Larry was on his way. If they had seen him in that town earlier you would breathe a sigh of relief and say "gee that's great". If you had Larry on your team, football or singing, it was worth a few points on the board before the others could start,' according to Jimmy.

The broadcaster had many rugby, hurling and soccer stars as well as Gaelic footballers on his All-Stars teams over the years. Both Larry and Jimmy say there are many funny stories about their travels and times with the different players. But for the sports broadcaster one of the funniest tales of all is about how a black English soccer player became linked with 'Lovely Leitrim'. Jimmy claims it's a true story.

'West Bromwich Albion soccer club was managed by Irish international player Johnny Giles when this incident happed. There were four or five other Irish players on the club's books at the time. They included Paddy Mulligan, Mick Martin, Ray Treacy and Giles himself who was a player-manager. He signed a player named Laurie Cunningham, a black man,' recalls Jimmy. He later played for a short time with Manchester United, 1982-83. West Bromwich signed Laurie around the time of his 21st birthday in 1977. He probably did not know the sort of jokers he would have to deal with among the Irish members of the squad.

Jimmy takes up the story about how the two Cunninghams, the singer and the soccer player, became inextricably linked. 'Ray Treacy was a real joker in the dressing room. As Johnny Giles was introducing this new black player to the others he came to Ray and told him who he was. Ray stuck out his hand and welcomed him saying, "Laurie, I have all your records, "Wicklow Hills", "Lovely Leitrim" and all the others." The new player hadn't a clue what he was talking about. But from that time onwards he became known among the other players as

"Lovely Leitrim"', adds Jimmy.

Laurie was the first black player to play for England at senior level while he was still under 21. In 1979 he was transferred to Real Madrid for a fee of £995,000. But even in sunny Spain this black player could not lose his 'Lovely Leitrim' label. 'In Real Madrid they also called him "Lovely Leitrim" even though they hadn't a notion in Spain where the nickname originated,' says Jimmy.

Sadly, Laurie died in a car crash in Madrid at the age of 33.

Playing With the Greats in the USA

Jimmy insists that it was apparent from the start of the All-Stars teams that the 'Lovely Leitrim' Larry Cunningham had the stamina and the physique to be a difficult player to mark.

'He was the sort of player that I would not like to be playing on for an hour. He was what you would call a sticky corner back. He was bony, and he still is bony. When you would go up for a ball with him, he would put you off your stride. When you run into a bony player you suddenly realise what you've hit. You hit his knee or his arse or his elbow and the end result is that you end up without the ball,' claims Jimmy.

'Larry was a competitive player and he wanted to compete with people such as Dermot O'Brien who was on our very first team too. But he was only nine years after winning an All-

Ireland medal so you needed to be good to keep up with him. Dermot was still near enough to his heyday as a player. Frankie Byrne who won All-Irelands with Meath was there as was Dublin player Jim Tunney who later became a TD, Government Minister and Lord Mayor of the capital. In later teams we had other All-Ireland players such as Dublin's Jimmy Keaveney, Sean Doherty, Paddy Cullen and many other All-Ireland stars. Larry was well able to play alongside them.'

Larry says he has memories of playing alongside some of these greats in the sweltering heat of Las Vegas. It was on a day when many of the team said that it was too hot to play. But according to Larry they were told by Jimmy to tog out, as they had never failed to play a game anywhere, irrespective of the weather.

Jimmy agrees that this was one game that was almost too hot to handle! 'On that day in Vegas the sun was so hot it would split the desert! But there was one tree providing a little bit of shade on one side of the field. Jimmy Keaveney said to me before we went out that he would like to play at left half-forward. I said that would be fine with me. Then at half time he came up to me and he said that he was thinking it would be nice if he could play at right half-back for the second half. It was only then I realised what he was up to. He wanted to be playing in the shade of the tree. He was a wise man!' insists Jimmy.

Larry also says that playing with some of Ireland's greatest inter-county players during another American trip was one of the highlights of his football days. Every year the GAA would send inter-county teams to America for the Cardinal Cushing Games, organised by the late John Kerry O'Donnell. They would play games in New York's Gaelic Park, as well as in pitches in Boston and Hartford, Connecticut.

'In Hartford we were playing in a strange type of pitch operated by an American softball team,' laughs Larry. The reason they were over there at all was because the late John Kerry O'Donnell had one of his regular rows with the GAA authorities in Ireland. That year they officially stopped a team of inter-county players from going out to the USA to play in the games. However John Kerry wanted the games to continue and he called in the help of his friend the broadcaster Séan Óg Ó Ceallacháin.

'Séan, who was a great player himself, suggested to John Kerry that he should contact me. He came up with the idea that the Jimmy Magee All-Stars play in the States as a replacement team. We agreed to do it and Larry was very much part of that team. It was such a massive success. It raised more money than any of the conventional Cardinal Cushing Games when county teams played in the States,' recalls Jimmy.

He had hall of fame footballers on the team as well as the showband people such as Larry and Dermot O'Brien. Other players on the team in 1971 included Kevin Armstrong of Antrim, John Nallen of Mayo, Sean Purcell and Frank Stockwell of Galway, the great Cork hurler Christy Ring, Gerry O'Malley of Roscommon and many others.

There is a funny story which both Larry and Jimmy recall about how the great Cork hurler Christy Ring showed the

Americans how softball should be played!

'We were watching the Americans playing softball in Hartford, when the strangest thing happened involving the late Christy Ring. He was watching all that was going on in that game from under the shade of a tree when Jimmy Magee convinced him to join in,' says Larry.

Jimmy finishes telling the story in some detail. 'Christy was cute and he was taking stock of what those who were playing softball were doing. Some of our boys, including Larry, agreed it would be great to see Christy have a go at softball. But he was reluctant to get involved until I went over and convinced him to have a go. He had been watching them playing the game for about an hour so he knew everything that was going on. Christy was very smart yet he asked those involved how he should hold the bat, even though he knew damn well what to do. He asked them to get one of their best throwers to pitch the ball towards him. Ring hit it the same way that he would if he was playing in a Railway Cup final back in Ireland. The ball sailed over the wall, over the trees and down the motorway toward New York. He threw down the bat and said something like, "That's a home run, isn't it?" – and with that he left the pitch. One shot, that was Ring,' laughs Jimmy.

A Wiry Player

While Larry admits that he 'hasn't a clue' what amount of money was raised for charities over the years by the Jimmy

Magee All-Stars, the broadcaster says it is in the region of four million Euro. Larry says that all the money raised went to worthy charities and broadcaster Liam Campbell, who was in charge of the accounts, ensured that every penny raised was accounted for. Jimmy recalls that Larry was a playing member of teams right up to this millennium. 'Larry played longer than most. One could say that he has been playing football for as long as Jack Nicklaus has been playing golf,' laughs Jimmy.

But Larry claims that his last outing with the team was in a non-playing role. It was back again in Ballyjamesduff where it all started out decades earlier. 'On that final occasion when we got together in Ballyjamesduff it was only a get-together. The local GAA club honoured us at a function there. That was only a few years ago as the late Dermot O'Brien was home for that event. The All-Stars had run its course at that stage but it had ran a very successful and long course,' recalls Larry. His sentiments are very much in line with views expressed by Jimmy Magee in the interview in the *RTÉ Guide* back in 1991. During that interview Jimmy recalled how people told him when he started out that his All-Stars idea wouldn't last a week. 'They were right. It lasted 25 years,' he told Brian Carty in that interview. (*RTÉ Guide*, 22 March 1991, p.9).

Jimmy has great memories of many of the All-Stars getting together for a special TV show hosted by BiBi Baskin on RTÉ towards the end of their playing days. He recalls this was filmed in Ballinasloe, County Galway and among those interviewed for the *RTÉ Guide* magazine prior to the show by Brian Carthy was Larry.

In the course of that interview Larry remembered many of the games between members of the Mighty Avons and Joe Dolan's band, the Drifters. 'If both bands were performing at a carnival anywhere near each other, we'd meet beforehand for a game, and I can tell you it wasn't easy stuff either.'

Jimmy recalls that Larry put in such a punishing schedule on the road and in the studio, as well as playing football, that his energy amazed him. 'If a performer could do all that now you would say that he must be on something to keep him going. But Jesus! Larry was an amazing man. He was so fit, he was wiry and I think that's the best word to describe him,' Jimmy insists.

But the only drug Larry was on was cigarettes – which should slow him down rather than speed up his performance on the playing fields.

Sexual Encounters With Fans

Apart from smiling when he was being described as a 'wiry' footballer, Larry also laughs out loud about some of the tales of sex, drugs and rock 'n' roll from that era. He claims that some of these stories are little more than media myths. But it is a view not shared by others who were showband members during the swinging Sixties.

'Of course there were times when a few of us might have slipped out some back door or window of a dressing room to get home.' One assumes that this was to get away from some adoring female fan who might be waiting and perhaps hoping to get closer to the entertainers. But he says that in general all the fans wanted to do was to have a talk and get an autograph after the dances.

'Apart from a few times when we had to slip away quietly we were lucky enough that this was the sort of music scene we were working in,' he says. When asked to elaborate on this, Larry says that the music he was playing did not attract the 'groupies' coming to his door. 'The type of songs I was singing did not entice that sort of an audience. The ones coming to my door would possibly be a wife and husband or a boyfriend and girlfriend. Perhaps they might be on holidays and they might arrive to have a photograph taken at our house. I was lucky that the songs I was singing attracted that type of fan,' he replies.

This view seems to concur with sentiments expressed by showband and jazz musician Paddy Cole in an interview with Eamon Dunphy on RTÉ Radio 1. 'They were admirers rather than groupies. We were too busy practising and playing during those days and nights to get involved with fans. Anyway most of the fans that came up to us just wanted autographs,' recalls Paddy. (*Conversations with Eamon Dunphy* RTÉ Radio 1, 14 March 2009)

But other singers and musicians from the showband era have spoken and written about a much more promiscuous scene. The views expressed by both Larry Cunningham and Paddy Cole are very much at variance with those expressed by Derek Dean of the Freshmen showband. Many stories in his book, *The Freshmen Unzipped* (Merlin Publishing 2007) are about sexual exploits with adoring fans. According to that book, drink also played a part in the showband scene.

'We were lucky that most of us did not drink in the Mighty Avons during the early years. I would say that helped us a lot to work well together during those times. I was a Pioneer until I was 34 years of age,' adds Larry.

Another book about the showband years *Are Ye the Band?* by Jimmy Higgins (Mentor Books 2007) also suggests that the dancehall days were during an age of innocence. An earlier book from the 1990s, *Send 'Em Home Sweatin'* by Vincent Power, paints a similar picture. It too reflects an era of relatively little sexual or drugs-related interaction between fans and the showband stars.

Larry Cunningham admits to hearing stories about some priests checking cars parked outside dancehalls in an attempt to scupper the frolicking of some couples. On other occasions he heard about some men of the cloth checking inside the dancehalls to ensure that couples were not dancing too close together!

But how close did the showband stars get to their fans? Was it, as is portrayed in sections of the Derek Dean book, an era that revolved a lot around drink and of getting 'stiff' with the groupies? Or was playing with the Jimmy Magee All-Stars the biggest sideshow for many of the showband stars and their fans? Perhaps playing with the All-Stars was a safety valve for some singers. But were the dancing punters mostly autograph hunters and not sex-starved groupies anxious to have flings with their favourite singers?

One suspects it was a bit of both, even though Paddy Cole and Larry Cunningham would have us believe that all the fans were innocent autograph hunters!

Nine

Big Changes with Daniel O'Donnell's Man

I n a calm-before-the-storm scene, a shaft of moonlight projected an outline of a window frame, in silhouette, on a side wall of the Mayo ballroom. The moonlight illuminated the empty hall, now in semi-darkness. To quote a song title the scene really was one of 'Moonlight in Mayo'. But the stillness of the night was suddenly shattered by some loud voices reaching a crescendo. This cataclysmic event (in showband terms) in a Castlebar dressing room would help spawn Daniel O'Donnell's success decades later. The illuminated window outline on the ballroom wall looked strangely similar to the way a projectionist's light might display an image, albeit more clearly, from an 8 millimetre film. These home movie cameras were often used in schools and halls during the 1960s and 1970s to project images on to screens or white walls.

The tired-eyed roadie with Larry Cunningham and the Mighty Avons may have taken only a fleeting glance at the moonlight-illuminated mirage in the Mayo ballroom. Suddenly his attention was deflected from the moonlit image on the wall as the stillness was shattered by the loud argumentative tones coming from the dressing room. Mick Clerkin tried to take no notice of the voices getting louder as he packed away the guitars, speakers, amps and microphones into the band's bus. He had joined the group as road manager a few years earlier in London where he was working in a much less glamorous driving job.

Larry Cunningham says he vividly recalls Mick Clerkin as a fan who worked as a van delivery driver in London and who was a regular follower of the band. Mick remembers those times too, long before the row in the Mayo ballroom dressing room which changed everything. Mick remembers the band being a huge attraction in Mayo during his time as roadie with them. The dances in the Royal Ballroom, Castlebar were always packed to capacity. That was the situation on the night in question when everything changed for Larry Cunningham and the Mighty Avons.

Long Before the Row

The Mighty Avons initially offered Mick a job for a temporary period as they needed a road manager/driver for a tour of major UK venues.

Mick Clerkin takes up the story. 'I was working for a

company named Initial Towel Supplies. I was delivering roller towels to toilets and bathrooms in hotels, work places and major civic buildings – places such as Heathrow Airport, the Ford Motor Company in Dagenham, Selfridges in Oxford Street and other big outlets. I was also keeping an eye on what the Mighty Avons were doing on the dancing scene in England. The reason I followed the band was because most of them were Cavan men. The exceptions were Larry from Longford and Ronnie Griffiths from Monaghan,' recalls the Cavan native.

'I would go along to see them when they played in the London area, mostly in the Galtymore, Cricklewood and the Gresham Ballroom,' he adds. Mick was in the Galtymore Ballroom on the night that Larry and the band broke all records for a crowd of over 6,800 dancers there. 'I knew the home areas where the lads came from and I got to know them better at the dances in London. I wouldn't have known them very well before I left Ireland. My initial contact with them was by going up and saying "hello" to them after the dances. The late Brian Finlay was the first one that I became friendly with. He was the drummer in the band and he came from Cavan town. Anyway they were offered a tour of the UK, outside of the Irish ballroom circuit, right up to Glasgow. They asked me to take some time off work and drive them for the tour and that's how I first became involved with them,' recalls Mick.

Phil Solomen, who also promoted many major acts including the Bachelors who were popular then, promoted that tour. He was a big promoter in England and Ireland at the time. Later on he also had a record label, which had major success in England with another Irish country artist Frankie McBride.

'He provided the Mighty Avons with a coach for the UK tour but they had no driver and I was approached to see if I would do the job. They asked me if I would be in a position to get some time off work. I approached my boss and explained the situation to him. He was a nice enough guy and he said there was no problem as I could take some leave of absence from the job. As far as I can remember it was a three-week tour. It was Phil Solomen who had brought Jim Reeves into Ireland to tour a few years earlier and that was a bit of a disaster,' remembers Mick. Mick was not involved with the Mighty Avons at that time but he had heard all about them playing support for Jim at the controversial dance in Lifford, County Donegal.

A Job Back in Ireland

Neither the Solomen connection nor the show in Lifford years earlier had any bearing on Mick accepting temporary work with the band.

'After I finished driving them for that tour of the UK they told me they were having a band bus specially built in Dundalk. They asked me if I would be interested in driving them to all their gigs. I think it was Brian Finlay who asked me if I would have any interest in the job. Larry was not very involved with that aspect of the business then as far as I can remember. I just spoke to him the same as everybody else. But it was mostly Brian Finlay who I was dealing with even though Jimmy Smith was the leader and boss of the band,' recalls Mick.

The job offer as a road manager back home in Ireland was something that Mick had to think long and hard about. He had a wife and two children at that time as well as a steady job in London.

'I had to give it a bit of thought and I spoke to my wife at that time. She said that I should consider giving it a try and she was prepared to stay on in London for a while longer as we had a reasonably priced flat there. It would have been a big move for us all to go to Ireland together. Sometime during 1966 I came back to Ireland and got digs in Cavan town. Eventually the new bus arrived. Its arrival had been delayed and I think I had to wait around for a month or two. Anyway I started driving the band to the gigs but after getting this bus specially made for taking them everywhere they suddenly decided to take their own cars.

'They were hugely popular then and I was left driving around in this big tour bus mostly on my own. Lord has mercy on band member Paddy Smith – he would travel with me in the bus more often than the rest. But usually I was driving this big bus carrying a few musical instruments and the little bits of sound gear that they used on stage. When I see what Daniel O'Donnell has for his live shows compared to the few pieces of sound equipment that I was bringing around back then, I laugh. All they had were some speakers, amps and a few crazy boxes. As well as being the bus driver I would also set up, and take down all the equipment. Now there are technicians for sound and others for lights, people put up the rigging as well as drivers – it's a different world,' he claims.

Relationships Weren't Great

Larry Cunningham is reluctant to go into details about the deteriorating relationships within the Mighty Avons that resulted in him and the band parting company.

'We didn't part on the best of terms,' is all he will say. But Mick Clerkin is much more specific. 'I know it all came to a head after a gig in Castlebar. It seems they weren't agreeing on terms and Larry decided he had enough. They obviously had their own problems getting along together. I remember well the night of the Castlebar dance that was the beginning of the end. I was doing my own thing, packing the gear away in the bus and there was quite a bit of a row going on in the dressing room. Anyway, I was almost finished packing the gear away when Larry walked out of the dressing room carrying his suit in its cover. He said something like "it's all over, I'll be leaving them in three weeks time."'

Larry's next words took the rookie roadie by surprise. 'He asked me to call to his house on my way home that night.

Larry lived outside Granard on the road to Cavan and I was living in Cavan then. He told me that if I called to his house he would fill me in on what was happening. So I drove to his house in the middle of the night. We talked over several cups of tea and he made me an offer that was responsible for getting me into the management side of the business. He said that he wanted me as his new manager. But I declined the offer at first as I said to him that I wouldn't have the contacts. My response was that the only experience I had was driving the bus and putting up the sound gear and taking it down. But he replied that I had met a lot of promoters while I was with the band as I was also collecting the money each night.

'Most bands at that time were on a percentage of what was taken at the door. It was usually 60 per cent for the band and 40 per cent for the promoter. The Mighty Avons' manager back then, the late Charlie McBrien, rarely if ever travelled to the gigs. So my duty, after setting up the equipment at the venues, was to sit in the box office with the promoter and at the end of the night count the money. When I collected the band's takings I would then hand this over to Jimmy Smith before packing away the equipment into the bus.

'In the course of doing all that I would have met a lot of promoters and various other people associated with the business. Larry said that he also had a lot of promoters ringing him from America and that the USA would be our first destination if I took over his management. The Mighty Avons had an office in Cavan at the time which was only a short distance away from where I was living. Anyway he convinced me that night that I should go to the band's office on the Monday and hand in my notice as well. As you can well imagine relationships weren't great between Larry, myself and the rest of the band for the following few weeks,' remembers Mick with a wry smile.

Big Among the Irish in America

Mick continues, 'After leaving the Mighty Avons the two of us headed off to America and that was where we did our first bit of business. I phoned up some of the contacts that Larry had given me. They were mostly in New York and Chicago. Larry got bookings to sing with the resident bands at a few venues in these cities.

'When we were in New York he stayed with his sister for a week and I stayed with my sister who was also there. We then went on to Chicago where we did a weekend of dates for a promoter named Jim O'Neill who was a native of the West of Ireland. He had a travel agency, a ballroom, a pub and a club – all in Chicago. Larry was huge in America at that time among the Irish emigrants. There was only Larry and myself on that trip so it was just him out front with the resident bands in the venues that he played. There were no Mighty Avons members around but he still could draw the crowds even when singing with what were called house bands at the various venues,' adds Mick.

They came home and set up a new band, as there was a lot of demand for Larry to get back on the road in Ireland again. 'We called the new band the Blue Boys but that name had to be quickly changed to the Country Blue Boys. The widow of Jim Reeves, or her management, threatened to sue us if we continued to use the same name as her late husband's backing group. Larry was still signed to the London-based King Record label and he could not leave until his contract expired. Around the time of the split with the Mighty Avons, Jimmy Magee and myself set up Release Records. But we had to wait a while for Larry to join us after his contract with King expired. I could not get along with the lady in London who owned the King label. She had her own ideas which did not coincide with mine. So we set up the new record label in Dublin. But I knew we would have to wait for Larry because he was still under contract to King. As I did not get on well with the lady in the London record company I knew that if we broke that contract she would sue us,' he says.

Mick Clerkin is at pains to emphasise that without Larry Cunningham putting pressure on him he would never have been in the music and record business. 'It is important to note, that were it not for Larry, I might never be in this business. He did put pressure on me because he felt that I could do the job of managing him. Indeed I would go so far as to say that he insisted on me doing the job. This obviously convinced me because if he thought I could do it then I should give it a try,' suggests Mick.

Prestige But No Pay

Around the time that the partnership with the Mighty Avons was unravelling, Mick Clerkin was becoming involved in getting Larry on the first International Festival of Country Music in London.

'I had discussions with the promoter of the Wembley festival, Mervyn Conn, about Larry participating. We also discussed getting a record stall at the festival. Of course later on we got Ray Lynam and others on the festival. Mervyn Conn was, in my opinion, a very difficult man to deal with. We had to buy space for the record stall and he did not pay any fee to our artists at that time,' recalls Mick.

Larry praises Mick for his efforts on his behalf at the Wembley festival. 'Mick Clerkin was responsible for getting me into the London festival. The first year we played there I would estimate that about 3,000 to 4,000 Irish people attended and I was the only Irish act on the show. But for us to be allowed have a stall there selling our records, I had to play for free and we still had to pay something like £1,000 for the stall. However, as we sold a lot of records it was introducing us to new audiences,' says Larry.

But the early years at the Wembley festival were frustrating times for his manager. 'The American acts always got priority and later on I would frequently have rows with Mervyn Conn over the time slots. He might give Larry a half an hour slot but then some American singer could go yakking on and on and

Larry's slot would change. Some Americans would run over their time slot due to all the talking they were doing. This would result in the Irish acts being cut back in their time slot and of course I would go to Conn and have a row with him. It is my view that, initially anyway; he did not have a lot of appreciation for the Irish artists. But we eventually won some of the battles with him regarding the time slots and we got more time for our Irish singers. There was a big Irish contingent at the first Wembley festival and it was mostly due to Larry being on the show as he was hugely popular at that time. But he still got no fee and we had to buy the stand to sell our wares there. However Wembley was good exposure as a lot of record buyers attended the event. Apart from the thousands of Irish that were there a lot of the others were seeing Larry for the first time,' Mick adds.

Larry felt that promoter Mervyn Conn acted unfairly by not paying him to appear at Wembley during these early years of the festival. 'To me it wasn't right but if you wanted to make it on the country scene in the UK you needed to make it at Wembley. But after a few years we realised that we did not need to appear at the festival anymore and we gave it up. I played there with many of the major American artists of the time, George Jones and Tammy Wynette, Tom T Hall, Willie Nelson and others. There were always pre-concert banquets on Good Friday nights and most of the artists would attend them. Mervyn usually had a few of the biggest American acts performing at those functions. On one occasion we were at the table next to Tammy Wynette and George Jones. Mervyn would have a good band playing after the dinner and he would ask different acts to go up and sing a song. They didn't have to if they so wished. But I saw George Jones and Tammy Wynette going up to sing on the spur of the moment and they were great,' remembers Larry.

As time went by the reviews reported Larry gaining greater confidence playing at the Wembley festivals. His improved performances were noted in the prestigious British country music magazine *Country Music People*. But initially, the then editor of that publication, noted country music critic, Bob Powell, was less than complimentary of Larry's first Wembley appearance. 'Larry Cunningham and the seven piece Mighty Avons are one of Ireland's most popular showbands. But in spite of the fact that they feature country songs in their act they are a showband, and seemed out of place at Wembley.' (*Country Music People* May 1969).

However by May 1971 Bob Powell had changed his tune about Larry Cunningham in a review of that year's festival. 'Two years ago, Larry Cunningham impressed me not at all, but this year he was much, much better,' (*Country Music People* May 1971). By 1972 Larry was billed as one of the star attractions on the Sunday night show at Wembley, sandwiched between Bill Anderson and Tom T Hall. He was now being given equal billing as the major American stars and Canada's Anne Murray of 'Snowbird' fame. Larry was also among an elite group of artists invited back for the 20th anniversary of the Wembley Country Festival.

Nashville Here I Come

The possibility of using Wembley as a launching pad for success on the US country scene must have entered Mick Clerkin's mind around this time. He made valuable contacts with people in the music business in Nashville during those London concerts.

Mick says he was not involved in the music scene in earlier years when Larry and the band made their first US foray by appearing at Carnegie Hall. But he was managing Larry when the Longford man appeared at the prestigious New York venue again. That was in 1971 and at a time when Larry's manager was also looking towards the scene in Nashville.

Mick says that much of the credit for opening doors in Nashville must go to a man named Pat Campbell. 'He was a big name on Radio Luxembourg around that time. He went on to present a major country music programme on BBC Radio 2 for years. Pat was from Dublin and it was at the first Wembley Festival in 1969 that I met him. He introduced me to Tommy Hill from Monument Records in Nashville. At that time Monument had Kris Kristofferson and a few other big names signed to the label. A man named Fred Foster owned the label and when we got to know them they agreed to record Larry over there. Tommy Hill also worked with another label, apart from Monument and it was on this label that he promoted Larry's Nashville single "Good Old Country Music"'.

'Tommy had the contacts with many major radio stations in

the US and they felt that the song had a very good chance of being a hit there for Larry. It was a good up-tempo type of country song which got a great response from the listeners. People would phone in when we were on the various radio programmes and there was a buzz about it. I think that if Larry was in a position to live there it could have worked for him. To make it in America you need TV exposure and back then you needed to be based there. Larry was not interested in that and so we came home and concentrated on the scene here. As far I know Larry was the first Irish artist to record in Nashville,' recalls Mick.

But was the cost of recording in Nashville at that time astronomical? Mick says he can't remember.

'Those recordings probably cost a lot of money at the time. But all I remember now is that Tommy Hill was able to do some sort of deal for us at Monument Studios,' remembers Mick. However it was still a costly exercise as they used many of the top session musicians and backing vocalists.

Larry recalls, 'Mick Clerkin lived the music game. He knew the right people in the business and he looked for different avenues to promote an artist. The three albums that I did in Nashville were his idea. He knew the right people to go to there too. We had many of the musicians who worked with Elvis Presley.'

They hired members of the vocal harmony group The Jordanaires. They had a long and successful association with the recordings of Elvis. They feature on many movie scores and were Grammy award-winners in the mid 1960s.

Other top session musicians such as Hargus 'Pig' Robbins (piano) and Pete Drake (steel guitar) did not come cheap either. Drake played on music sessions with artists as diverse as Jim Reeves, George Harrison and Ringo Star of the Beatles as well as working with folk/rock superstar Bob Dylan. At one time he was reputed to have played on almost 50 of the top 75 songs in the US Country charts. So when Mick Clerkin says 'these people did not come cheap' for a recording session it is obvious this is true. But the standard of musicianship has stood the test of time. Larry's current record label, Ceol Music, recently repackaged some of these recordings and many music critics have written that there is still an outstanding quality about these tracks.

A County Councillor's Handshake!

Larry was very much in awe working with the top musicians in Nashville, especially people who were in the backing band used by Elvis. 'The first day I was in the Nashville studio when I saw the musicians that I was going to be working with I was as nervous as a kitten. They included top American musicians such as D.J. Fontana, Hargus 'Pig' Robbins, fiddle player Tommy Jackson, producer Tommy Hill, Jerry Shook and Lloyd Green. But I remember D.J. Fontana coming up to me and putting me at ease. He said that when a singer had come over 4,000 miles to record with them they were very proud. He said they felt honoured by this. According to him all they wanted to do was ensure that the end results would be the best possible recordings. He told me to relax and sing as if I was at a session at home,' remembers Larry who also has one very funny memory about that session.

As mentioned earlier, one of the songs that Larry recorded in Nashville, 'Good Old Country Music' was singled out as having hit potential in the USA. 'It was written by Porter Wagoner and he had also recorded it. I thought it was a great song but after I sang it in the studio in Nashville the producer was unhappy,' he recalls.

Tommy Hill asked Larry if he was sure that the words he was singing were correct, as he did not think they were. Larry's reaction was that it was too late to check them at that stage but the producer said that Porter Wagoner had an office nearby on Music Row.

'We went over to his office and told the receptionist our business. Eventually Porter Wagoner came out and he gave us what I would call a county councillor's handshake,' laughs Larry. In other words the handshake was devoid of any real feeling. 'Anyway he gave us the words and sure enough they were different to what I had been singing,' he adds.

Larry's 'No' To US move

It was due to the influence of producer Tommy Hill and recording engineer Scotty Moore that Larry's recording of 'Good Old Country Music' was played on some radio programmes in America.

'We got such a good reaction that they decided to release it as a single. Nobody knew who I was in America but once the song got a few plays the feedback was good. We were encouraged to go back to America and promote the song on five major radio stations. They were "larger than large" radio stations and they covered a vast area of America. We flew over again and in less than ten days we visited all those major radio stations and promoted the song. There was no question about it, among truck drivers in particular, the song had started to become hugely popular.'

While Larry claims the song could have been a big hit he was told that the only way to ensure that happened was to go and live in the USA. 'I wouldn't leave Ireland at that time for all the tea in China so unfortunately that is as far as success in the US went.' He is hesitant as he muses over the might-have-been success for his career in America. 'I know well, Oh! I can't really say that I know well, but I imagine, that if I moved out there it could have happened,' he adds.

Recording with the top names in Nashville helped Larry get a spot on the early morning TV programme *The Ralph Emery Show* which was screened daily from Nashville. 'It was a huge show; similar to the big morning TV shows that we now have in the UK in particular. These shows that are hugely popular now such as GMTV and others are similar to what Ralph's show was in the USA all those years ago. Americans are usually ahead of the posse and they had big morning TV shows long before they were anywhere else,' states Mick Clerkin.

Larry also remembers that he got a good response on that show. 'But I thought it was very strange going in before 6 a.m. to work on that TV show. We rehearsed with the Willburn Brothers backing band for about 5 minutes before the show. They were so good that in a few minutes they knew the backing music for both of my songs. The backing sound that those boys got in such a short time was so good it was almost unbelievable,' he recalls.

Larry also appeared at the Country Music Convention Week in Nashville in October 1971. According to sleeve notes penned by Pat Campbell of the BBC for Larry's album *Songs Fresh from Nashville* – he got a big reaction there. 'How they acclaimed him, a standing cheering ovation, which gave my Irish heart a lift it hasn't had in years,' states Pat.

Larry also got on well when he appeared on the Grand Ole Opry. 'It was great to get on that show and I remember that Bill Monroe and his Bluegrass Boys were top of the bill that night,' recalls Larry. Bluegrass legend Bill was the man who wrote 'Blue Moon of Kentucky' which was on the 'B' side of the first hit by Elvis Presley. Mick Clerkin also says that Larry's Opry appearance, at the old Ryman auditorium, was a high point of their Nashville trip.

Larry Leads to the 'Discovery' of Daniel!

Did his work with Larry in the USA and England pave a path that made it easier for Mick Clerkin to steer Daniel O'Donnell towards international stardom later on?

'Well there were a few other artists that I was also involved with as far as UK success was concerned, before Daniel came along. I didn't stay too long in the management side of the business with Larry as it wasn't really my scene. The late Barry Cline took over from me in dealing with booking the live dance dates. I was more interested in the record side of the business and still am,' states Mick. He is now boss of Daniel's label Rosette Records. After initially setting up Release Records he and Jimmy Magee were lucky to have big artists from that era, including Larry, involved with the label.

Mick Clerkin says Larry, who was always a builder, was even involved in building the premises at Lombard Street, Dublin which housed Release Records for many years until the demise of the label. 'We were also doing record distribution from there but it eventually became a difficult business and it didn't stay the course. I was getting very frustrated with the small size of the Irish market and that was one reason for me moving on. I always wanted to have a go at the UK record market as I felt that country and middle-of-the-road or folk artists were not getting a fair slice of the business there.'

In 1981 Mick's new label Ritz Records had a massive hit in the UK pop charts with 'Sweet Sixteen' by the Furey Brothers and Davey Arthur. Later on in the 1980s his record label steered 'Bunch of Thyme' by Foster and Allen into the UK Top 20.

'The Fureys as well as Foster and Allen got on *Top of the Pops* which was great exposure for them. Both acts were very successful all over the UK. I feel that if Larry's "Tribute to Jim Reeves" had been with a bigger label 20 years earlier it could have been a Number One or at least a top five record in the pop charts in England,' claims Mick.

Larry Cunningham says one British-based, Irish-born radio presenter was instrumental in getting his records, and those of other Irish artists, played in the UK. 'Any time that BBC presenter Terry Wogan got a chance he played our records on radio in the UK. He became a great friend of Mick Clerkin and this helped many Irish artists. A mention from him on his radio programme still carries a lot of weight among radio listeners in the UK. I'm sure his radio plays helped Daniel O'Donnell in the UK after Mick discovered him,' suggests Larry.

Mick Clerkin agrees and he says he 'discovered' Daniel O'Donnell in 1985. He has worked with him on the recording side of his career ever since, but Sean Reilly has been his manager.

'Apart from the time I spent managing Larry I never again got involved in artist management. Daniel did not have much going for him at the time that I first signed him to a recording contract. He kept coming back to me and asking me to get involved financially in the management of his live shows. I was out of Ireland at that time and discussed the matter with my friend Sean Reilly. I was delighted when he took over Daniel's management and the rest is history,' he smiles.

Mick Clerkin, who has steered the international recording career of Daniel O'Donnell, is in no doubt about how big Larry Cunningham could have been internationally too.

He claims that Larry was one of the biggest showband stars of all in his time. 'I am convinced that if he moved to the States he could have been a massive success there. After Jim Reeves had passed away there was nobody doing his sort of stuff. Nobody ever went down that musical route again. Larry was capable of following in Reeves' footsteps in the States if he wished. But he would have had to go and live there at that time. It is very different now as Daniel is promoted there by PBS TV and he can also go over and do regular concert tours without having to move there permanently,' concludes Mick.

In his mind's eye, and ear, Mick Clerkin must often wander back to that fateful night in the Castlebar ballroom when Larry Cunningham threw him a music management lifeline. But the noisy exchanges in the dressing room, remain more indelibly etched in his memory than the artistic image projected on the ballroom wall by the moonlight in Mayo!

Ten

Looking Forward – Looking Back

Looking forward. Looking back
I've come a long way down the track
Got a long way left to go
Makin' songs from what I know.
— Slim Dusty ('Looking Forward. Looking Back'
written by Don Walker 2000)

Over lovely Leitrim the blood red summer sun was sinking low. The hearts of showband fans were sinking too after a tragedy unfolded on a road near Carrick-on-Shannon on a July day in 1975. Two nights later shots rang out as the starry, starry night sky struggled to illuminate a dark, bloodied, stretch of road not far from the Mountains of Mourne. Down along that County Down road the triple murder of musicians further rocked an already reeling showband business to its core. Decades later thoughts of his music career ending amid fears of throat cancer and heart failure loomed large in Larry Cunningham's life.

Then once again his mind must have raced back to July 1975 and the day (and night) that the (showband) music died for many. These were times when, in the minds of many, one musical genre died. But it was a different one to what Don McLean sang about in his Buddy Holly inspired 'American Pie'. Ironically he sang about starry, starry nights and 'The Mountains of Mourne' too.

Larry Cunningham claims 29 to 31 July 1975 were the darkest days and the nights in Irish showband history.

The sad events started on 29 July when Tom Dunphy of the Royal and Big 8 showbands died in a car crash near Carrick-on-Shannon, County Leitrim. He was en route to a dance date in Donegal. Two nights later three members of the Miami showband were murdered near Newry and these sad events will remain forever etched in Larry Cunningham's mind.

'Tom Dunphy's death hit fans very hard in Ireland, England and America. He was a personal friend of mine and of my former manager Mick Clerkin. I felt so sorry for his wife and family and for Brendan Bowyer too. He was Brendan's right arm in the band business and they had worked so closely together over the years. Only days later the Miami murders really shocked me as I had played the previous weekend in the same ballroom that they played in on the night of their deaths. But for the grace of God it could have been us who were massacred. It seems those involved were targeting a showband. And that could have been any showband. We were playing at a carnival in Monaghan the day that Tom Dunphy died and our gig was in Bundoran on the night of the Miami murders. These are two dates that I will never forget and for all the wrong reasons,' recalls Larry.

A Head-to-Head in the Charts

Larry admits that he entertained dancers across all religious divides in Northern Ireland. 'Fans from all religions, and none, come to see me perform right up to the present time. If one goes back to the origins of the Mighty Avons the members were living near Ballyhaise which is a border area. Among the first gigs we got were ones playing in Protestant halls. It was great to get the work then and they always paid us well so there were no problems. As time went by and our records became successful, the North became an even more important part of our life. I remember that after 'Lovely Leitrim' we seemed to become very well accepted in the Six Counties,' claims Larry.

But he says that the real catalyst for his popularity in the North was the success of his follow-up to 'Lovely Leitrim' – the Johnny McCauley song 'Among the Wicklow Hills'. Johnny is a Derry-born singer-songwriter who has lived in London for most of his adult life. A chance visit to a record shop in Derry resulted in Larry buying an EP by Johnny which contained some of his original songs. Among the tracks on that EP were 'Pretty Little Girl from Omagh', 'Among the Wicklow Hills' and 'Cottage on the Borderline' which were all massive hits for Larry. The other track on the EP '5,000 Miles Away from Sligo' became a hit for Big Tom many years later. Johnny McCauley also wrote one of Big Tom's biggest hits 'Four Country Roads'. Later on he wrote 'My Donegal Shore' the song that launched the recording career of Daniel O'Donnell.

The sequence of Johnny McCauley-written hits for Larry began with 'Among the Wicklow Hills' – but it nearly didn't happen. Larry remembers that they were desperately seeking a follow-up hit to 'Lovely Leitrim' when this song emerged. He says they had given it to producer Noel Kelehan with a view to recording it. They were also 'trying it out' at the dances. But Larry claims that somebody involved with the management of the late Gerry Cronin and the Ohio Showband from Tuam had similar ideas.

He remembers that the Mighty Avons got an urgent call from the record producer to come into the studio quickly. They were told to get it recorded immediately as Eamonn Andrews Studio had also been booked to record Gerry Cronin's version. 'We had a head-to-head with this song in the charts. But thankfully for me our version won the chart battle,' recalls Larry.

For Larry the commercial success of 'Among the Wicklow Hills' in the North was phenomenal. 'The first order from our distributors in Belfast was for 15,000 copies. I remember that in the whole 26 counties there were barely 15,000 copies of the song in the shops at the same time. The North was also first back for second orders of the single. To this very day the North is a very important corner of Ireland for me. Unfortunately about 1968 I saw the first sandbags in cities there as violence erupted. There were a lot of things done that I'm sure people on both sides of the border are sorry for today. But I prefer not to dwell too much on it now. Sadly for a time during the height of the troubles in the North we completely stopped playing there,' he sighs.

Feeding the Baby Amid News of Band Murders

Larry continues, 'I remember the weekends being big for dancing in Banbridge, County Down. But some roads leading to and from the town had double gates on them at that time. At 3 a.m. those gates were locked and if you had not left the area by that time you had to stay on until later in the morning.

'The big rush after we finished playing there around 2 a.m. was to get the gear packed and get out. I remember my manager, the late Barry Cline, doing most of the driving after those gigs. From Banbridge he would head for the nearest point across the border which was Dundalk. We had to drive through a section of the road which was very dark, and one night before the Miami tragedy I remember my remarks to Barry. I was half asleep during the journey when I said that this was the sort of place you could almost expect an ambush to happen. His reply was that if I had nothing better to say I should go back to sleep. But unfortunately only one week later at that very spot the Miami were ambushed. I announced on the night that we played there that the Miami would be the big attraction in that ballroom one week later,' he remembers.

It was about 2.30 a.m. on 31 July 1975 when the Miami showband members were heading back to Dublin from their gig in the Castle Ballroom, Banbridge. They were flagged down at a roadblock near Newry. They thought it was a routine British Army or RUC checkpoint. It emerged later that as members of the Ulster Volunteer Force (UVF) tried to load a bomb into the band bus it exploded prematurely killing two of the UVF members.

The plan seems to have been that the bomb would go off later as the band were nearing Dublin. The UVF could then claim that the band were involved in bomb smuggling. But when the bomb exploded at the scene the other UVF members opened fire on the Miami musicians. They killed singer Fran O'Toole, guitarist Tony Geraghty and trumpet player Brian McCoy. Bass player Stephen Travers was seriously injured but survived. So also did sax player Des McAlea (Des Lee) who was blown over a ditch by the force of the explosion.

'After that I did not go back working in the North for years and it is only about 10 or 12 years ago that I felt comfortable again playing in the Six Counties. One of the first major gigs that I did again in the North was for top promoter David Hull. It was in the Waterfront Hall in Belfast which wasn't even there during the time of the Troubles,' he adds.

Beatrice also had some anxious moments at home in Granard on the night that the members of the Miami were murdered. 'At that time a lot of Larry's business was in the North and I knew that he had played a week earlier in the same hall where the Miami played their last gig. I remember sitting on the side of the bed feeding one of our babies when the report about the ambush came on the 6 o'clock News. I was anxiously waiting for Larry to arrive home from playing. I remember saying it to him when he arrived home and it was a major shock for him. It could have been him or any other showband that was in the wrong place at the wrong time that night.

'After that Larry and the lads did not play much in Northern Ireland. Any time they did I would be worried for him and the musicians who worked with him. All of those lads had families and we felt responsible for them too. It was a difficult time in Ireland but thank God we lived to see it all change. We go to the North very often now and there are countless devoted fans of Larry's there. They are the loveliest people and Larry is accepted so well by them that it is just brilliant,' says Beatrice.

Popular Northern bandleader Jimmy Johnston sums up the reasons for Larry's popularity in the Six Counties. 'Larry was around the dance circuit when my own band, The Jimmy Johnston Showband, was also touring the country six nights a week. His big appeal up North came when he released 'Lovely Leitrim', mostly I think, because we have Leitrim up here in County Down. Many people in this area associated the song with this local townland. Even to this day Larry is a very popular singer in the North, especially in County Down. He will always remain one of Ireland's true country legends,' says Jimmy.

Carnivals Were the 'Bread and Butter'

In the 26 counties Larry Cunningham has memories of playing to massive crowds at many carnival marquees. One of the biggest marquee crowds of all was at Ballygar on the Galway-Roscommon border in 1966. According to a book published to mark the 60th anniversary of Ballygar Carnival, Larry and the Mighty Avons created a crowd record there which was never equalled.

'The year was 1966 and Larry from Granard was at the top of the charts with his song 'Lovely Leitrim'. It was a night that anyone who was there will never forget. The town was brought to a complete standstill. The management team at the carnival had to put the emergency plan into action by ensuring that no more than 2,000 patrons were allowed into the marquee. The remaining 1,000 were forced to watch and listen from outside the perimeter fence. Larry will never forget the night in 1966 when he entertained 3,000 fans both inside and outside the carnival marquee in Ballygar.' (*Ballygar Carnival Anniversary Book,* p.79)

However Larry is not certain if this was the biggest crowd that he ever played to at a carnival marquee. 'Ahem! It would be one of the biggest anyway. But there was a carnival in Stradone, County Cavan and it was a toss of a coin between it and Ballygar regarding the biggest marquee crowd we ever entertained. There was another carnival in Piltown, County Kilkenny which was in a nine-pole marquee. We had some of our biggest dancing crowds there also. In Ballygar I remember that the carnival marquee was in a large enclosed field and once you got inside the gates you had paid your fee and you were in the entertainment enclosure!

'I remember another carnival that was also nearly as big as Ballygar and it was in Leitrim, County Down. It was near the home areas of the great Down footballers Sean O'Neill and Paddy Doherty. I remember playing there in a three-pole marquee which was sitting in the middle of a big field. Long before we went on stage, I believe before we even arrived at the gig, the place was packed with dancers at 9.30 that evening. God rest my manager Charlie McBrien, he discovered early on that no more would fit into the marquee. So he got members of the local football team to stand at the ditches around the field. He then went to the gate leading to the field and opened a makeshift box office there. The man who told me this afterwards was at the dance that night and he paid to get in at the field gate. He said that by the time he arrived at the sides of the marquee they had been lifted up to let in fresh air. It was packed to capacity inside. But he was a big fellow and he pushed his way in through the crowd. However as soon as I came on stage there was a surge forward by some of the dancers and the crowd lifted him out of the marquee and he couldn't get back in. When he went up to the entrance of the tent again they wanted to charge him a second time. It seems that he got no admission ticket at the makeshift box office at the field gate earlier,' exclaims Larry with a loud laugh.

As the showband scene expanded in the 1960s Larry

suggests there were times when some shady practices were used by a small number of managers and bands to get their records into the hit parade. 'Getting into the charts meant more people coming to the dances and the higher a record went in the charts the bigger the crowds were at the live gigs. It was obvious that after six or seven years of compiling the Irish charts that some bands and their managers would have an idea which shops might be surveyed. As soon as some artists and managers started buying their own records it was a disaster for the whole business.

'The late Eddie Masterson, who wrote the "Tribute to Jim Reeves", contributed a column to *Spotlight* magazine and he wrote a funny article about this on one occasion. I remember reading Eddie's claim that he witnessed the manager of a well-known band with his car parked beside the River Liffey and the boot open. Eddie questioned the manager as to the round black plastic discs that he was throwing into the water! It seems that this happened and it did no good for the business,' adds Larry.

Among the many highlights of Larry's career was playing for Princess Grace (Kelly) and her husband Prince Rainier of Monaco during their state visit to Ireland in 1961. Larry and the band played for the royal visitors at Powerscourt. This was a major charity event which was attended by society people from Ireland and abroad. Larry and the boys purchased white *báiníní* (traditional old-style Irish jackets) for playing at this special event.

'Powerscourt and the surrounding grounds looked

unbelievable. We were there in an upper room looking down at red carpets and £100 dinners. Some of the ladies were wearing dresses that were a mile long!' recalled Larry with a laugh on the RTÉ TV programme *A Little Bit Country*. (RTÉ 1, 29 October 2006).

'Powerscourt was one gig I will always remember but I can't recall even a fraction of all the places around Ireland that we played at carnival marquees. Now when I drive through some towns and villages I suddenly realise that we may have played at a carnival in some field there years ago. I see the remains of many big ballrooms too where we had good gigs on Saturday or Sunday nights. But when we wanted to play the other five nights the carnivals were the venues for us. They were the bread and butter of our business back then,' claims Larry.

Don't Let Me Cross Over That Cliff!

Driving in winter through snow and frost to and from distant dance dates does not hold many happy memories for Larry. Playing (music) for the famous Kerry footballer Mick O'Dwyer had its downside during one wintry night as Larry explains.

'Mick had a venue in Waterville which is no nice journey from Longford in bad weather. My manager at that time was the late Peter Sheridan. The date in Kerry was during some of the worst Christmas weather that we ever experienced. I believe there was about six inches of battered snow on most roads and we were sure that the dance in Kerry would be cancelled. Indeed I was thanking God that we would not have to make such a long journey in bad weather.

'But, about four days before the gig, Mick O'Dwyer phoned Peter and said he hoped everything was OK for the dance. Peter asked him if he was serious as the roads were so bad that it seemed unlikely that we would be able to get as far as Waterville. However Mick replied that we would have to get that far as they had no snow around that area of Kerry. It seems that due to Atlantic weather conditions, and perhaps the Gulf Stream, there was about 20 miles around Waterville that had no snow at all that Christmas. So as the dancers down there had no problem getting to the hall therefore we had no option but to be there.

'It took us 10 hours to make the trip and even though we stayed over it was the following night before we were back in Longford. The four tyres on our bandwagon were in a shocking state after the journey. We had to drive along the rough margins of the roads for much of the journey. We lost a set of tyres as a result of the Kerry gig. Perhaps I should have followed Mick O'Dwyer for the price of new tyres as well,' suggests Larry with a smile.

On another occasion Larry came close to taking a serious tumble down a mountainside when his car skidded off the road while driving over the Curlew Mountains. But there was a funny side to his slide off this mountainside.

'While I was climbing the mountain it was OK but when I began to descend towards Boyle that was where it was most dangerous. I was only crawling down this slippery road when the car started to skid into the verge. Beyond this was a small wall of loose stones, only about two feet high. Beyond that it was a 40 feet drop into the valley below! I was powerless as the car pushed a large section of the stones over the edge and the front wheels also slid over. The middle part of the bottom of the car balanced precariously on the remainder of the loose stones.'

Half of Larry's car was suspended in mid-air over the mountain ledge. The wheels stopped spinning but the radio kept on playing. 'I eased myself into the rear seat as gently as possible and opened the back door to get out. Ironically as this was happening the song playing on the radio was my version of "Don't Let Me Cross Over"', laughs Larry.

Protest March

Larry remembers being among a number of entertainers on a protest march to the Dáil and Radio Éireann to try and get more airplays for Irish records. He recalls at that time the situation in Britain was that the BBC played about 80 per cent of songs by UK artists.

'Unfortunately it was the opposite here in Ireland as the national broadcaster was playing 80 per cent foreign records then. We got occasional spins from some friendly presenters such as Larry Gogan, Jimmy Magee, Gay Byrne, Peter Murphy and others when they were allowed to do so. But radio plays were very few and with no pirate radios or local stations we decided to protest in Dublin.'

Looking back on it now Larry suggests that the lack of airplays may have been a blessing in disguise. 'When people could not hear enough of us on radio they came out to hear us at the dances and that helped pack the halls. However a large group of us marched to the Dáil and Radio Éireann. I remember that Brendan Bowyer and myself, as well as the late Ronnie Drew of the Dubliners, were among those leading the march.'

Decline of the Dancing Scene

Larry recalls that he saw a drop-off in crowds attending carnival marquees long before the attendances at the big breezeblock ballrooms started to decline. He claims that both the singing pubs and, slightly later, the disco scene, hit the dance halls hard.

'Christy Maye in Mullingar was the first man that I remember doing discos. He had a record player, speakers and LPs and that was the first time I saw people paying to hear somebody play records at a dance. Everyone laughed at the idea at first but it gathered momentum and others followed his example. He is still involved in the business and some time ago I played for him at a Mike Denver concert which he promoted,' he adds.

Larry feels that ballroom owners should have moved faster to make their venues more comfortable for the patrons. He thinks that if they did, the scene could have competed better with the discos and the singing pubs and it would have lasted longer.

'Dance halls were the cheapest form of entertainment venues to operate. They were little more than four walls, a roof and a dance floor. The provision of toilets and dressing rooms were afterthoughts. Hotel and bar owners eventually realised that they could capture some of this dancing business. All they needed to do was put in some new carpet, soft seats, a large dance floor and book small music groups. This is what they did and that was the beginning of the end for the dance halls. But the ballroom owners could have taken similar action long beforehand. If they got bar and restaurant licences then the dancing scene might have lasted another ten years.'

In 1971 Larry Cunningham had his last No 1 with 'Slaney Valley', a song written for him by Paddy Kehoe of Glencarrig, Enniscorthy, County Wexford. He was the father of the famous Wexford hurler Padge Kehoe. His next biggest hit, 'My Kathleen', spent 14 weeks in the charts in 1975 and reached number 3 in the summer of that year. It was to be his most successful chart entry during the mid-1970s. Even though a re-released 'Lovely Leitrim' came back into the Top 20 in 1974 it peaked at a lowly number 19.

In 1974 he headlined a concert at London's prestigious Royal Albert Hall. Margo (O'Donnell) and the late Joe Lynch (later 'Dinny' in the TV series *Glenroe*) were the main supporting acts. As the 1970s went by Larry Cunningham and his Country Blue Boys joined forces with Margo for a brief spell during the middle of the decade. In 1976 they had a Top 20 hit titled 'Yes Mr Peters'. It was a cover version of a song popularised in the USA by Loretta Lynn and the late Conway Twitty.

'I joined with Margo for three or four months, even though neither of us needed the other to draw big crowds. However the attendances we attracted together were almost unbelievable,' recalled Larry. (*A Little Bit Country* RTÉ 1, 26 October 2006). On the same programme he recalled their biggest crowd of all. It was on their opening night at the Casino Ballroom, Castlerea, County Roscommon. Larry remembers he had to abandon his car about half a mile away from the hall as the town was so packed with the cars of fans going to the gig.

Larry and Margo also had a best-selling album during this time. But the partnership did not last long and the Country Blue Boys also moved on with Margo leaving Larry without a band. 'The manager and myself had to get a new band together very quickly. We got some of the original Mighty Avons, who were not working at the time, as well as a great musical couple Chuck Owens and June McLoughlin. In a matter of days we had a new band on the road,' said Larry. (*A Little Bit Country* RTÉ 1, 29 October 2006).

As the 1970s slid into the 1980s the slide in business and in record sales for showbands became evident to everyone. But Larry had several Top 30 hits right up to his last one, 'Galway and You' written by Mayo man Michael Cummins in 1983. However, he did not grace the elusive No 1 spot or the Top 20 again during his recording career.

Retiring a Few Times!

Even though he fronted several bands up to the late 1990s, Larry Cunningham also retired from the business on a number of occasions. Still the lure of the stage proved too great for him and he consistently made comebacks, some of those with the original Mighty Avons.

The most successful comeback was in 1986 when the eight members from the early days did a memorable six-week comeback tour. The band got rave reviews during that tour and one published in the *Evening Press* was typical of what was written in the newspapers about Larry and the lads. The story stated that babysitters made a fortune that night as couples headed out to relive their courting days. 'Mr and Mrs Ireland put on their dancing shoes and stepped out to welcome Larry and the Mighty Avons in Dublin's National Ballroom.' The story, by Helen Quinn, stated that 20 years after 'Lovely Leitrim', Larry and the band still had that magic touch. 'The 1,500 capacity crowd, eager for a binge of their favourite Sixties' country and western hits, weren't disappointed. From the moment they took to the stage the Avons had them hip swinging and hand clapping beneath the spinning mirrored globe'. (*Evening Press*, 4 October 1986).

Larry and the Mighty Avons were to tour again a few years later but sadly at that stage some of the original members had passed away.

When his neighbour and former ballroom owner, Albert Reynolds, went for election as a TD in 1977 Larry campaigned for him. Later on when Albert became Taoiseach he was still a loyal supporter of his. But Larry had little interest in politics and he quickly eased out of that scene. 'Some of what I saw happening in politics, involving all parties, I did not like. It certainly would not be my idea of a career.'

However he enjoyed being one of many showband stars that were guests for a day at Áras an Uachtaráin in 2001. As she welcomed the stars on that occasion President Mary McAleese said she was a fan of the showbands during her younger days. 'The last time I was in your company I was looking for a good-looking fella' with a car to give me a lift home,' she joked. (*Irish Independent*, 11 July 2001)

In the same story the writer Eugene Maloney states that Larry Cunningham was also a favourite of the President's mother. But talking to reporters at Áras an Uachtaráin, Larry played down his importance as a star from the showband era. 'Larry recalled how in Roscommon in 1997 a young girl approached him for his autograph. He told her, "Go home, love, your mother has it already." (*Irish Independent*, 11 July 2001).

Heart Problems and Fears of 'the Big C'

It was during the 1980s that Larry started to play more at concerts and on cruises abroad. 'The late Noel Henry from Mayo, who was very successful in the band business in the USA, was the first to book me to perform on a cruise ship. At the time I was doubtful about doing this as I did not know what sort of an audience one would have on a cruise ship. However I gave it a try and discovered that it was mostly people of my own age and younger that were on those luxury liners. There were as many as 3,000 emigrants and Irish-Americans on several cruise ships that I entertained on. After doing six or seven of these cruises, some from Miami and others from Mexico and Bermuda, I started doing them here in Europe.' All of Larry's entertaining on cruise ships is now in Europe, mostly in the Mediterranean. He is also a regular performer at concerts for Irish people in holiday hotspots in Spain, Portugal and the Canary Islands.

Larry and Beatrice laugh when they recall a recent incident when he was one of the guest stars at a week of shows on the Canary Islands. 'After one of the concerts a nice mannered young lady approached me for an autograph. She was probably in her mid-30s and she said she had enjoyed my part of the show. Then she added that it was great to hear me singing live, as she never had that experience before. I replied to her that she nearly missed me!' says Larry with a laugh. He was referring to recent bouts of ill health and how she could have missed seeing him perform live if doctors and modern medicine hadn't saved his life.

Just as his career was enjoying a renaissance during the new millennium he was hit by a number of health scares. The first one was a throat problem, which emerged after he started to encounter a lot of hoarseness during some of his concerts abroad.

'I was smoking at the time and while I was reluctant to give up the cigarettes I had little option but to do so. My doctor sent me to a specialist and after various tests I was told that there was a white coating on one of my vocal chords. He said that he had never seen anything like this before and I thought that this was the end of the line for me. Even though he said that he had not seen any similar condition before, I felt he probably had. My reaction was that the big C (cancer) might be facing me. It was ten days before the doctor could get me into hospital. During those days I cancelled everything for the following two months and to be honest I didn't expect to ever sing again.

'But thank God the doctors were able to deal with the problem and having monitored it for another 12 months the hoarseness never returned. Another result of the medical treatment was that I ended up with a lower note than I ever had before. Since then I can hit a higher note as well,' he says. Even after being off cigarettes for over two years Larry suddenly started to experience heart problems.

'I was threatened with a heart problem but luckily enough before it got too serious the doctors did something about it. I had to go to the Mater Hospital in Dublin where I was under the care of two great doctors, Dr Hurley and Dr McCann. They carried out a triple bypass, which resulted in me being back home in a short time and in great form. However, about two years later I decided to have another angiogram just to see if all the tubes that had been put in earlier were still working! They discovered that I had an aneurysm, which required immediate attention and that was dealt with then. But a few years later it was discovered that I had another one and I had to go back into hospital again for further treatment. That was a few years ago and thank God since then I'm in great form. I hope it stays that way,' says the singer who remains on Warfarin medication to keep his blood thin due to his recent history of heart-related incidents.

Now in his 70s Larry remains the same thin and hardy man that he has been all his life – 'wiry' as Jimmy Magee once described him. He does not seem to be suffering any ill-effects from his heart and throat scares during the past decade.

The Lost Generation of Fans

In 2009 Larry Cunningham is still as enthusiastic as he was back in 1959 about putting on the best possible performance every time he takes to the stage. But he is a realist too. The singer, who does not want any of his children involved in the music business, believes it is tougher than ever for young acts today. Larry was very outspoken about this on a radio interview on Galway Bay FM two years ago. He had just performed before a full house at a concert given by a younger singer. But while Larry said the age profile of the crowd was perfect for him, more young fans were needed for younger singers to survive. 'A lot of the crowd that were clapping along to my songs tonight were there dancing to us 40 years ago. If that is the future, then is there a future for the younger singers of today?' he asks. (*Country Crossroads* Galway Bay FM March 2008).

When questioned about his observations during interviews for this book Larry was slightly less outspoken. But he still displayed lingering doubts about the future for young Irish country artists.

'The last thing that I would want is to see this business going down the tubes. If anyone told me in 1959 that 50 years later myself and others from those days would still be singing, we would not have believed them. But what hit the younger generation of country singers hardest was when discos took over in the 1970s. A person approaching 40 today might never have danced to a showband. This is despite a great crop of new younger country singers coming along since then – including stars such as Declan Nerney, Mick Flavin, Mike Denver and others. Of course they all have their own fans but unfortunately they have to also depend on some of ours who have been loyal followers since the showband days. Lucky enough for us, all those fans from the showband era are still out there dancing and supporting us both at home and abroad. But I would love to see more of my age group encouraging the younger ones to try this type of music and also showing them how to dance,' he smiles.

'I would be happier if we had more of the younger generation attending our dances and concerts and performing on stage as well. They are the future, we are not, we have our job done,' he adds. Would Larry want any of his grandchildren following in a showbusiness career? 'Well I don't think that I will have any say in that. But with the way the music business has gone it will be a big problem to know what is going to happen next for the live music scene,' he replies.

Regrets? . . . Larry Has a Few

One regret that Larry has is that he never tried to break into the music scene in Australia. 'I have a sister still living there and she reared her family in Australia. She sent me the record of cowboy songs that helped start me off on a career in country music. I got several offers to tour in Australia but in the early days with the Mighty Avons America seemed a better place, and a nearer place, to play.'

'Travelling to Australia was costly then and whether it would have resulted in us making any money was another big question. Once I reached the 1970s and was fronting different bands I had other things happening in my life. The changes in the scene here diverted me from going to tour in Australia. However, I always had thoughts of going there for a tour, mostly because my sister lives there. But I've never got around to making that trip,' he sighs.

He also regrets that he did not take more time off touring when making some of his albums. He claims he 'cringes' now when he listens to some of the 'rushed' recordings that he made in the early days.

'When I toured with Charley Pride he told me he would take up to three months off the live scene when working on an album. If I looked for three days off I would be in big trouble. We should have taken more time in the studios when making some of those albums because a record is something that is there forever,' he adds.

Like another Irish-born entertainer, Val Doonican, still performing into his early 80s, Larry Cunningham has no plans to retire. The showband scene was shattered for him, but it did not die, when his colleagues were tragically killed in July 1975. Larry comes across as a man who is humble about the strange quirks of fate that made him a showband legend in his time. One suspects that showband success was something this singing carpenter never wanted.

Like everybody else he has visible human frailties too.

One challenge for an interviewer is his penchant at times to talk almost incessantly about everything from sport to carpentry when questioned about his music career! At times his recollection about highlights from his showband successes can be hazy too. However that is where his wife Beatrice comes into her own – displaying an amazing ability to remember days and dates, facts and figures. Behind every great man there is a great woman, or so the adage states. Larry is lucky that his wife Beatrice helps keep him on the road today. Not alone does she pack his case for shows in Tenerife, Tullamore, the Canary Islands or Carrick-on-Shannon but she is usually there backstage unobtrusively supporting him. Perhaps that's another reason why he is 'happy as Larry' (to quote another adage) not to retire. Why would he quit when Beatrice, and the fans, still encourage him to do what he loves doing.

'When no one comes to our live shows I will have no option but to quit. But that has not happened yet. So I'm still playing and I will be as long as the good Lord spares me,' concludes this ageless star from Ireland's showband era.

His wife smiles and one detects from her body language that Larry's longevity on the music scene is something they both still savour.

Makin' sense of what I've seen
All the love we've had between
You and I along the track
Looking forward. Looking back.

– Slim Dusty ('Looking Forward. Looking Back' written by Don Walker. 2000)

Selected Discography of Albums by Larry Cunningham

Album: *The Two Sides of Larry Cunningham* (Larry Cunningham and the Mighty Avons)
Label: King (Ireland & UK); Coral (USA).
Year: Ireland & UK: 1966, USA: 1967

Album: *Larry Cunningham Sings* (Larry Cunningham and the Mighty Avons)
Label: EMI (Talisman – Shamrock Series).
Year: 1968

Album: *Larry Cunningham at his Best*
Label: EMI
Year: 1969

Album: *Larry Cunningham – Forty Shades of Green*
Label: EMI
Year: 1970

Album: *Larry Cunningham – A Ramblin' Irishman*
Label: Release
Year: 1970

Album: *Larry Cunningham Remembers Jim Reeves*
Label: Release
Year: 1971

Album: *Larry Cunningham Sings Songs Fresh from Nashville*
Label: Release
Year: 1972

Note: The above three albums were all recorded in Nashville, Tennessee, USA

Album: *Larry Cunningham in Concert*
Label: Release
Year: 1973

Album: *Good Old Country Music*
Label: Release
Year: 1974

Album: *Yes Mr Peters* (Larry Cunningham & Margo)
Label: Release
Year: 1976

Album: *Just For You*
Label: K-Tel
Year: 1977

Album: *Irish Startime*
Label: Release
Year: 1978

Album: *This Is Larry Cunningham*
Label: Homespun/Outlet
Year: 1979

Album: *Silver Anniversary*
Label: Ritz
Year: 1989

Album: *Where the Grass Grows the Greenest*
Label: Ritz
Year: 1990

Album: *As Happy as Larry*
Label: Hazel Records
Year: 1995

Album: *From Nowhere At All*
Label: Ceol (Also released in the UK on the Prism Leisure label)
Year: 2004

Album: *Larry Cunningham's Ireland*
Label: Ceol
Year: 2005

Album: *Real Country Music*
Label: Ceol
Year: 2008
(This last album is a double CD of songs recorded in Nashville in the 1970s and recently re-mastered)

DVD and Video
DVD: *Larry Cunningham's Ireland*
Label: Ceol
Year: 2005

The Chart Hit Singles

Tribute to Jim Reeves	1964
I Guess I'm Crazy	1965
There's that Smile Again/Lovely Leitrim	1965
Among the Wicklow Hills	1966
Snowflake	1966
Fool's Paradise	1967
Three Steps to the Phone	1967
The Emigrant	1968
(All with the Mighty Avons on the King label)	
El Tigre	1968
Pretty Little Girl from Omagh	1969
Don't Let Me Cross Over	1969
Mother the Queen of My Heart	1970
Pride of the West	1971
Slaney Valley	1971
4 Great Irish Hits (EP)	1972
4 Great Irish Hits (EP) Vol.2	1972
Goodbye Comes Hard to Me	1973
This Time of the Year	1974
Lovely Leitrim *(re-released)*	1974
My Kathleen	1975
Yes Mr Peters (w/ Margo)	1976
Annaghdown	1976
(All on the Release label)	
The Story of My Life	1983
Galway and You	1983
(All on the Ritz label)	

Bibliography

Books

Allen, Bob (ed). *The Blackwell Guide to Recorded Country Music*, Blackwell 1993.
Carthy, Brian. *The A to Z of Country & Irish Stars*, Gill and Macmillian/RTÉ 1991.
Coughlan, John (ed). *The Swingin' Sixties Book*, Coughlan Publishing 1990.
Cowley, Ultan. *The Men who Built Britain*, Wolfhound Press 2001.
Davis, Paul. *George Hamilton IV – Ambassador of Country Music*, HarperCollins 2001.
Dean, Derek. *The Freshmen Unzipped*, Merlin Press 2007.
Gogan, Larry. *The Book of Irish Chart Hits*, Maxwell 1987.
Higgins, Jimmy. *Are Ye the Band?*, Mentor Books 2007.
Hurst, Jack. *Nashville's Grand Ole Opry*, Abrams 1975
Power, Vincent. *Send 'Em Home Sweatin'*, Kildanore Publishing 1990.
Streissguth, Michael. *From a Moth to a Flame – The Jim Reeves Story*, Rutledge Hill Press 1998.

―∾∾―

Newspapers and Magazines

The Anglo Celt
Ballygar Carnival Anniversary Magazine
Country Music People (London)
Evening Herald
The Evening Press
Irish Independent
The Irish Press
The Irish Times
The Irish Post (London)
The Irish World (London)
Leitrim Observer
Longford Leader
Longford News
Daily News (New York)
RTÉ Guide
Spotlight Magazine
Spring 3100 (New York Police Department Magazine)
Sunday Independent
The Tuam Herald

―∾∾―

Websites

www.accessmylibrary.com/comsite5
www.carnegiehall.org
www.guardian.co.uk
www.kgkireland.com
www.iangallagher.com/country
www.iangallagher.com/mightyavons
www.manhattan.about.com
www.nyc.gov/html/nyc.com
www.nytimes.com
www.theofficerdown.com

Index

D
Dean, Derek 170
Dean, Jimmy 147, 148
Denver, Mike 207, 214
Dixies, The 65,
Doherty, Paddy 201
Doherty, Sean 164
Dolan, Joe 155, 158, 159, 168
Doonican, Val 216
Doyle, Danny 20
Drew, Ronnie 206
Dubliners, The 20
Dunphy, Eamon 169
Dunphy, Sean 20, 144
Dunphy, Tom 146, 155, 195
Dusty, Slim 193, 217
Dylan, Bob 186

E
Emery, Ralph 188

F
Fitzgerald, Richard, 14
Flavin, Mick 214
Foster & Allen 191
Fuller, Bill 106, 107, 109, 111, 112, 115, 125, 126, 136, 137, 139
Furey Brothers 190

G
Gallagher, Liam 137
Gallagher, Noel 137
Gallowglass Céilí Band, 14
Galtymore, The 128, 133, 134, 174
Galway Bay FM Radio, 46, 213, 214
Garland, Judy 119
Giles, Johnny 162
Ginnity, Noel V 144, 145
Glover, Dave 35
Godfrey, Arthur 118
Gogan, Larry 56, 205
Goodman, Benny 119
Grand Ole Opry 9, 120, 189
Grace, Princess 202